REIGNING *Resilient* QUEENS

You Are Not Alone

GENESIS GOMEZ

Dorie McCleskey, Gabby Gonzales, Heather Brooke, Jenna Janisch, Kalena Rodriguez,
Karleen Wagner, Laura Farley, Lauren Jurkas, Marta Spirk, Shantelle Bridges,
Stacey Sanders, Tammy Green Garner, Whitley Nabintu Marshall, Whitney Watts Hays

Foreword by Christine Beckwith

Copyright © 2024 by Genesis Gomez

All rights reserved. No part of this publication may be reproduced, distributed, or transmitted in any form or by any means, including photocopying, recording, or other electronic or mechanical methods, without the prior written permission of the publisher, except in the case of brief quotations embodied in critical reviews and certain other noncommercial uses permitted by copyright law. For permission requests, contact the publisher at the website address below.

Reigning Resilient Queens / Genesis Gomez—1st edition
Resilient Royalty Publishing
https://reigningresilientqueens.com

The information contained in this book is for general information and entertainment purposes only. The recommendations, opinions, experiences, observations, or other information contained herein is provided "as is," and neither the author nor publisher make any representations or warranties of any kind, express or implied, about the accuracy, suitability, reliability, or completeness of this book's content. Any reliance a reader places on such information is, therefore, strictly at their own risk. All recommendations are made without guarantee on the part of the author and publisher. To the maximum extent permitted by law, the authors and publisher disclaim all liability from this publication's use. In no event will either the authors or publisher be liable to any reader for any loss or damage whatsoever arising from the use of the information contained in this book. This book is not a substitute for professional services, and readers are advised to seek professional aid in the event of an emergency.

ISBN: 979-8-218-51102-9

Praise for
Reigning Resilient Queens

"*Reigning Resilient Queens* feels deeply relevant. The book resonates profoundly with the message that no matter how difficult your past may be, resilience and personal growth are attainable.

The resources provided are another standout feature. They are practical, offering readers not just encouragement but tangible steps to seek help in areas like domestic abuse, therapy, or addiction recovery. These resources might be particularly helpful for women who are still in the midst of their own struggles, offering them a lifeline of support beyond the emotional inspiration the stories provide.

This book doesn't sugarcoat the pain or downplay the trauma; it validates it while simultaneously offering hope. The emphasis on community and sharing experiences is something that feels deeply necessary in a world where women are often told to carry their burdens silently. Overall, the book's concept of sharing raw, authentic stories combined with practical resources makes it an invaluable tool for anyone who needs the courage to continue on their path. It reaffirms that you are not alone, and offers a reminder that no matter the challenges you face, you too are reigning resiliently."

~Paris Byrum

"Brave. Bold. Powerful. The stories are told in vivid detail that at times can be hard to read, but they are so important. Too often we hide away those things that are difficult to talk about; too often we ignore the truth of our past. Every life is filled with challenges that at times can leave you feeling alone. There is strength and comfort in the act of sharing our experiences, it's a core part of being human. A powerful and inspirational read that is also relatable while emphasizing love and compassion for others and for ourselves. Each story showcases real life in an honest and profound way.
~Jennifer Carter

"*Reigning Resilient Queens: You Are Not Alone* is not just a collection of stories; it's a testament to the strength and determination of women who refuse to be defined by their struggles by sharing their experiences.

These women offer hope and encouragement to others, demonstrating that no one is truly alone in their Journey.

Their stories are a beacon of light showing how giving back to society can be a fulfilling and transformative experience.

I was personally captivated from the first paragraph to the last word and could not put this book down until I finished reading it."
~Dora Sherry, Radio Host at "People Helping People" and author of *Reflections of an Angel* and *The Path Of Awakening*

"A collection of first-person experiences guaranteed to uplift and inspire by demonstrating true courage, unimaginable strength, and complete resolve even when facing the most difficult challenges life can present."
~Ryan Henderson

"This book is truly fascinating. It enthralls you with stories of incredible women from all walks of life who find strength, peace, and purpose through some of the most unthinkable situations you could find yourself in. It is inspiring and empowering. No matter who you are, where you come from, or what you have been through, there is a story for each of us here."

~ Samayra Romano

"Reading this book's personal stories of resilient women makes me think of the many wonderful women I have met on my life journey.

The language is straightforward, powerful, and purposeful. It proves that anything is possible by just believing in one's strength. It's also believing in a higher power and placing trust in God, knowing that there is a bigger purpose.

This book is a great read for those struggling with their own challenges and purpose, and for those considering a career in the mental health field."

~ Bernadette McCann

I have cried, I have smiled, I have had "*I felt that*" kind of moments reading this book This is something that *everyone* should read! Very powerful.

~ Bobby Mercer

"Each story highlights different trials and tribulations from childhood trauma, sexual abuse to domestic violence, addiction, and much more. The stories are riveting, empowering, and relatable. They are accompanied by therapeutic excerpts that delve into the psyche of each experience in order to identify the mental health consequences of each trauma.

I found myself grappling with different emotions while engaging with this book. At one point I would feel tears creeping up in my eyes, while at other moments I felt anger and eventually hope. The book caused me to reflect within myself and my own journey. I felt empowered knowing that I am not alone. These women have inspired and motivated me to continue with my own healing."

~ Lucy Salas

"What resonated most for me was the message to breathe from Laurie Jurkas' chapter because it seems like such a simple concept and yet in times of difficulty and darkness it's the one thing we forget to do. "

~Krystle Rowe

"*Reigning Resilient Queens: You Are Not Alone* is a powerful anthology that showcases the indomitable spirit of women facing extraordinary challenges. What makes it truly remarkable is the raw vulnerability with which these women share their experiences. From tales of abuse and near-death experiences to struggles with fertility and the complexities of adoption, each story peels back layers of human resilience. This compilation is not just a collection of individual stories; it's a tapestry of human spirit and determination. It serves as a powerful reminder that adversity, no matter how daunting, can be overcome. For anyone seeking inspiration or struggling with their own challenges, *Reigning Resilient Queens* offers a beacon of hope. It's a testament to the strength of women and the transformative power of sharing our stories. More than just a good read, this book is a celebration of the human spirit and a call to recognize the resilient queens among us and within ourselves."

~Billy Montana

"This book is an encouraging, uplifting read! I definitely recommend if you're looking for a refreshing take on "self-help" books. There is a nice variety in the authors' styles, stories, backgrounds, etc. And it's easy to pick up and read a chapter at a time, as you have time."

~Jenna Hoskinson

"I think it's really good. It drew me in really well and it was a really good mix of emotions and inspiration. The book is written in a way that's relatable to people who have experienced somewhat similar things but also to people who haven't."

~ Tim Phillips

Dedication

To my beautiful children, who have seen more ups and downs than their poor little hearts should have had to endure, who have shown me the true definition of unconditional and true love, and who challenge me to be a better version of myself in every single way. "The purest form of love you could have given us is working on yourself!"- My daughter

To my nieces, nephews, and un-biological kiddos, whom I have taken under my wing at one point or another, both here and gone too soon—I love you so much and wish you all nothing but peace and happiness.

To my grandmother, for giving me a strong, powerful woman to look up to and want to emulate. I don't really know where I would be without your love, both tough and caring.

To queens who have had unwavering faith in this calling and felt in their hearts that this was a true calling from God—thank you for walking alongside me. I know this was not easy; I am not easy. But it is so worth it for the lives that will be changed by this movement.

To that little girl who was so scared, felt unworthy, and unsure why she was even born, but had big love in her heart, hope, and belief in herself, and faith in the vision God put on her heart. We have done it, sweetheart! You are doing it! You should be ever so proud of yourself, my love.

To God for giving me a calling and vision that has been with me since I was a little girl. Though it's been heavy and sometimes frightening, I've answered the call. Let's go! Let's grow!

Contents

Foreword xiii

Welcome xvii

Reflections of Resilience: Seeing Beyond the Surface 1
Genesis Gomez

This Little Light of Mine 13
Dorie McCleskey

Self-Love 25
Gabby Gonzalez

A Journey from Heart Bondage to Freedom 37
Heather Brooke

Fire Starting 51
Jenna Janisch

Halfway Dead 63
Kalena Rodriguez

I Have Good News, and I Have Bad News 73
Karleen Wagner

The Power within the Ordinary 85
Laura Farley

Breathe & Let It Be: Let Your Purpose Be
Greater than Your Pain! 95
Lauren Jurkas

Finding My Note: A Story of
Resilience and Redemption 107
Marta Spirk

Hiding in Plain Sight: A Quest to Be Seen 117
Shantelle Bridges

There is Light in Every Day 129
Stacey Sanders

A Journey to Completeness: Navigating
the Adoption Maze for Our Little Miracle 139
Tammy Green Garner

Embracing True Beauty: A Journey of
Resilience and Purpose..153
Whitley Nabintu Marshall

Dare to Be Different 161
Whitney Watts Hays

Acknowledgments 169

Foreword

To be a queen of anything, you need to feel like a queen. To feel like a queen, you must have an undeniable drive inside you that tells you daily you are worthy. I can say with 100 percent conviction that Genesis Gomez, the creator of *Reigning Resilient Queens*, has the secret ingredient and then some. Never have I ever looked at her from a distance or even up close and not thought to myself that she was here on earth to do something superior to most of her peers. She is a standout in the world around her in every measurable way.

I have had the honor of sitting with her for many hours, days, months, and years observing her. What I know is she has a grit that you cannot cut with a knife, and when provoked, it has the strength of a thousand lions. She will not be sidelined when it is her time to reign. And yet, there is something incredibly fragile and relatable in her presence, where you know that her matriarch heart bleeds and feels the pain at an amplified level. Those are the qualities of greatness.

See, one cannot be without the other. You cannot serve with a deeply and tremendously knowing and caring heart unless you open yourself up to the tragedies of the world and life. And you cannot overcome and rise out of the ashes of your own ruins like the phoenix without surviving great injury.

In the pages of this incredibly well-thought-out jewel, you will take a journey into the minds of warriors. Warriors who, at their height, have slayed a thousand dragons in their individual worlds. "Genesis" means "creator of worlds" or "new generation." So, living up to her name, she is here to help others "come into being of something" great.

This book is the body of work of someone who has shed her skin and accepted her seat on the throne. Not because she has anointed herself as royalty but because the world has made her a reigning and resilient queen.

Are you ready for your own crown? Follow the leader. They say there are only two ways to avoid mistakes in our futures: to learn them ourselves the hard way or to listen to others. This book will help you avoid dire mistakes and find the footpaths and footholds to greater heights. You simply need to sit back and allow the words and lessons to carry you beyond your wildest dreams.

Foreword

Christine Beckwith

CEO and Founder of Vision for Success Coaching
Author of the books *Wise Eyes, Clear Boundaries,
Breaking the Cycle, Win or Learn, Finding Honor*

Keep Up with Christine

https://www.facebook.com/visionyoursuccess.net

Welcome

Welcome to *Reigning Resilient Queens*, a book born from the hearts of women who have faced life's greatest challenges and emerged not just as survivors but as empowered leaders—queens in their own right. This book is more than a collection of stories; it is a testament to the unyielding strength, courage, and resilience that women possess. It is a celebration of the power of community, the importance of sharing our journeys, and the profound impact one woman's story can have on another.

The Reigning Resilient Queens movement was created with a singular mission: to uplift and empower women by providing a platform where their stories of triumph over adversity could be heard, honored, and celebrated. In a world that often tells us to be quiet, to shrink ourselves, or to fit into predefined molds, this movement boldly declares that our voices matter, our experiences are valuable, and our stories have the power to change lives.

This book is a reflection of that mission. Within these pages, you will find the raw and authentic stories of women who have faced seemingly insurmountable obstacles—whether it be personal loss, health challenges, discrimination, abuse, suicidal ideation, or tough choices causing moments of self-doubt—and they have risen above them with grace and determination. These women are not just participants in a movement; they are beacons of hope and resilience, lighting the way for others who may be navigating their own storms.

Each chapter is a journey into the life of a queen who has chosen to share her truth, not just as a means of healing herself but as a way to heal others. These stories are filled with moments of vulnerability, strength, and, ultimately, triumph. They serve as powerful reminders that no matter how dark the night, there is always a dawn.

The Reigning Resilient Queens movement also recognizes that true empowerment comes from nurturing the whole person—mind, body, and spirit. That's why this movement extends beyond storytelling to offer support, guidance, and practical tools through our strategic partnerships with Built to Recover, My Pain His Purpose Ministries, K. Project Freedom, The Billy Montana Company, Empire Beauty Schools, D20 Photography, Unleash Your Inner Author, Competitive Edge MMA, Model Mindset Mastery Services, 20/20 EyeVenue and more. This holistic approach ensures that women are not only sharing their stories but are also equipped to continue growing, thriving, and making a difference in their communities.

As you read through these pages, may you find inspiration, comfort, and a renewed sense of purpose. May you see yourself in these stories and recognize the queen within you. And may this book serve as a reminder that you, too, can rise above any challenge, reign over your life with resilience, and inspire others to do the same. Please make sure you have a notebook or journal ready to jot down notes, craft your action plan, and set your goals and dreams in motion for living your best life.

Welcome to the world of Reigning Resilient Queens. This is our story, and it's only the beginning. *You* are *not* alone!

Trigger Warning

This book addresses themes that may be triggering for some readers, including but not limited to trauma, violence, sexual and other types of abuse, addiction, mental health struggles, and experiences of incarceration. While our intention is to foster understanding and resilience, we acknowledge that these topics can evoke strong emotions and may be difficult to engage with.

We encourage readers to prioritize their well-being and seek support if needed. Please take care of yourself as you navigate these narratives.

Reflections of Resilience: Seeing Beyond the Surface

Genesis Gomez

"I can be changed by what happens to me. But I refuse to be reduced by it." —Maya Angelou

They say you have to be able to look at yourself in the mirror and be proud of the person looking back at you. What happens when you share the face of someone who was supposed to protect you and ended up hurting you beyond comprehension? How does one overcome hating the face that looks back at them? How do you find a way to be okay with yourself when all you feel is disgust and shame? If you can't look at yourself, how can you learn to love yourself or find yourself attractive? Worthy?

I saw his face every single day I would look in the mirror. "You look just like him," I would hear growing up. I hated my own face so much that I would scratch the fuck out of it with my nails on the days when I was so overstimulated that my skin would crawl and I hurt all over my body. The cutting and scratches released this pain somehow. Even for a fleeting moment, it seemed worth it at the time. Scratching my face would alleviate the comments of me looking like him, but I would get the comments, "What's wrong with you?" "You're so crazy!" And I felt it! I felt like reality couldn't be what it was.

I was always a talkative child. Since I was able to put sentences together, the story goes, I would talk to everyone and everything about whatever! I wanted to make friends no matter where I went, to the point I would talk to the store mannequins and get sad when they didn't talk back.

But it doesn't stop me from reaching out when I feel prompted or saying what I feel I need to say! This trait can and has gotten me into trouble. Sometimes, there's no nice way to say something. While I have gotten better with "If you have nothing nice to say, don't say anything at all," I'm gonna do my damndest to find a nice way to say what needs to be said!

I grew up begging and pleading for my mother to leave the man she chose to have children with. I would tell her, "It will be okay! I'm smart and capable; we will figure it out, I promise. I will find a way to make sure we're okay. You just have to get us out of here! You have to make the first step!"

This is one of my first memories of when we lived in Panama. I hated him! He made me so uncomfortable! I just knew if we could get away that we would be okay. You see, she was the lesser of two evils, it seemed at the time. He abused her as well, and unfortunately, she wasn't very bright. I saw she struggled a lot day to day, so I tended to make excuses for her. I wanted to take care of her. I wanted to make sure she knew she was loved and seen and heard even though she couldn't give that to me in return.

I felt so deeply that God sent me to her because I could take it. I could handle the abuse from him, and her, and the babysitters, and being bullied at school. In my mind, even at a young age, I felt in my heart I was going through what I was going through for a reason. I just didn't realize what exactly that was. I had this vision I held onto. It wasn't until I grew older that I began to realize the impact her enabling of his behavior, words, actions, and abuse had on me, and why I felt the need to protect her, my brother, my sister, and didn't really give a shit what happened to me.

She also brought her own abuse to the table. She would tell me she loved me, but she would also tell me how much she despised me, how she wished she never had me. In fact, she wished she would have given me to that nice rich white doctor family or, better yet, aborted me when she had the chance. Then, she would proceed to state how she wished I would just kill myself.

In my adolescence, I woke up in the middle of the night to her with a knife to my throat. She had a wild look in her eye and said, "I just wish you would fucking die." I was so scared, but I just felt like she was having an episode. I talked her down and got her back to bed.

They had episodes of kindness and love and fun mixed with episodes of terror and hatred and agony. It just seemed like they didn't mean to, him included. They wouldn't ever apologize. It was just, "What are you talking about? That never happened."

If you are paying attention, yes, I am, in fact, talking about my parents. You know, the people who are supposed to love and protect you. Yeah. Ha. Those people.

Listen, I know I've said a lot of sad and scary shit. If you're still reading this chapter without putting the book down and saying, "Fuck this! What the hell?" Good for you! You're not gonna be disappointed.

Normally, I start off with a rather cute story of how I was born and was almost declared legally dead. The doctors broke my nose, stuck a needle through my tongue, and I was connected to all these tubes. Just as the doctors were gonna give up on me, as the story goes, it was then my dad called my mom and asked her to marry him, and I started breathing again! "She's alive!" So, I got the name Genesis as the beginning of the family. I finish with inflections, and I smile a half smile and nod my head. Telling it this way is usually followed by, "Aww, how cute." And then I'm the subject of people saying, "Hey! You've gotta hear the story of how she was born! So cute!" *Yea … cute until …* But I don't always go into the story as I've told it here. Well, I haven't until more recently when I decided to finally answer the calling God placed on my heart long ago.

My childhood was not horrific all the time. There were fun times. There were hugs, and lessons to be taught, and conversations had. There was just enough good that I really did believe I made up all the bad. I truly believed that I was delusional and dramatic and that I just wished things were awful. This is what was explained to me by my parents when I tried to make sense of reality. I would try to talk about it with other people even though I was told not to. If I felt safe, I would talk. That, coupled with bruises and cuts, was enough to have Child Services at our house often. But not enough to get us taken away. We were the pillar-of-the-church, God-fearing, Christian family when Child Services people were around. And I was just a disturbed drama queen who would get my brother and sister "all worked up for no reason." I was a "fakalater" (their nickname for faker). I accepted this but wanted to desperately change myself. *What was wrong with me?* I had an overabundance of love to give! I wanted love! But I was also so angry and would react poorly when trying to stand up for myself or my brother or sister. I was not okay with disrespect or gossip or abuse, donning the name "Katie Kaboom."

I would do my best to forgive my parents and myself. After all, it says that in the Bible, right? Also, we must honor our father and mother! "But they're your parents …"

I believed I was such a problem. I was bullied at home, bullied at school. I was such a weirdo, but I did find people who would show me kindness. I felt like they saw the real me, but they could never stay. Either they moved or I moved, the nature of the beast being a military brat and being from a poor family. When he got out of the military, he couldn't hold down a job and neither could she. So we moved a lot then too.

The way he got out of the military is a story in itself. I was around six years old. I was waking up to get a glass of water. I came into the living room to find my dad on top of my aunt. He was laughing and she was crying and scared, trying to fight him off. She mouthed to me, "Help me!" I was standing there frozen and scared. He looked at me anxiously and yelled, "Go to bed, pervert! This is none of your business! You're next!"

And I ran and hid myself under the covers. My memories are often referred to as "popcorn memories" as they tend to have a very clear vision followed by a dark black space, and then another vision hours or days later. The next clear memory is being at the military police station to be questioned. I remember going into a room by myself and turning to the hallway to see my mom wearing sunglasses, holding my sister, with my brother sitting next to her and my aunt next to him. My aunt was looking directly at me as they closed the door. These two grown men with angry faces and tones of voice were asking me question after question! I just remember hearing, "That girl out there is promiscuous. She was trying to come onto him. She has messed with your mind to think he's done something to you! He is a good soldier, a good man! He wouldn't do this, and by you testifying that he did, you're ruining his life! You're ruining your life and your family's life! You don't want that to happen, do you? Now, Genesis, tell us the truth. He didn't actually hurt you or your aunt, right? You girls are just making up stories for attention, right? So we are going to ask you one more time. Did he rape you or your aunt?"

With tears in my eyes and a crack in my voice, I said, "No." They looked at me with lips pinched, half smile, nod of the head, and they let me out of the room. As I walked out, it was like she knew I let her down. My heart sank. I felt like such a failure. I felt so weak, and I was so disappointed with myself. It felt so heavy. There are many pivotal moments in my life, and this was certainly one of them. *"How could I be so weak?"* I thought to myself as I sat in the chair beside her. *My aunt has never let me live that moment down.*

Some of you reading this may have just said, "But you were just six years old." Yes, I finally came to that conclusion and eventually forgave myself. But I held an incredible amount of guilt and shame and responsibility for far too long until I was able to let it go enough. Writing this is a reminder of how far I have come because I remember the pain I held in my body. I remember the anger, the guilt, the shame, and the resentment, but I have finally reached a place where I no longer hold space for this. I think we are at a point in the story where I want to provide notable moments, good and bad, and then get into the "how" since I'm often asked how I turned out the way I did through all of this.

Early Memories:

I remember that men and women older than me and schoolmates my same age were obsessed with my genitalia for some reason, while also making me look at or touch theirs constantly. This was an uncomfortable feeling—never was I ever curious! I hated every bit of it!

I remember my dad lining up my brother, sister, and me to have us watch him snap the necks of baby bunnies and just laugh. I also remember him throwing a dog across the room and beating it so badly that he killed it. I still just don't understand at all why this was necessary!

Having to care for my little brother and sister at a very young age because my dad was gone and my mom couldn't get out of bed from alcohol, drugs, depression, sickness—many reasons. I would do dishes, laundry, go to the store up the street, buy milk and eggs, and bring them home. I was around five or six. Can you imagine sending your five- or six-year-old to the store these days?

I remember playing at the playground by myself and dreaming of the life I wanted to have. Getting lost in the woods by myself and then bringing home pets (turtles, frogs, etc.).

Sliding down the hill on cardboard boxes over the pine needles and laughing and laughing.

Winning academic and art awards throughout school and being so proud of myself but also not believing it was true.

A friend who was a light in the dark. Shaunice lived across the way and felt so safe! I wish I knew where she was or how she ended up. I think of her often as she was a staple in my life.

I remember the lake and camping!

Road trips and sunrises, movies and parties, pool time, board games, and holidays!

Learning to work on my car, yes, he taught me that. I know how to change my tires, oil, serpentine belt, washer fluid, brakes—all from him.

I learned how to cook, sew, and draw from her. She is an incredibly talented artist and the epitome of wasted potential.

I remember having Christmases and birthdays because my grandparents (my dad's parents) would come to the rescue the best way they knew how and take care of us. They also even gave us a place to live and would pay bills when my parents couldn't make ends meet. In a lot of ways, they were our saving grace, and I do not know where I would be without the impact I allowed them to have on me.

All the good, the bad, and the ugly that my early childhood put me through set the stage of the good, the bad, and the ugly I would endure into early adulthood. I continued to find those who would gaslight, manipulate, physically and sexually abuse me. Until one day, I was so angry with life and with myself. I walked into a gas station while angrily praying and asking God for help. The water bottle I grabbed had a bracelet that stated, "Life won't change until YOU change your life!" Bam! It hit me!

I looked up and said, "Really, Bro?" (talking to God) and then, "Okay." I put that bracelet on and didn't take it off until it fell off. I started to work on my anger. I started working on knowing myself and not allowing people to make me think my reality wasn't real. I started cutting people out of my life left and right. I started going after what I wanted in life. I looked for opportunities and said yes to whatever I thought was going to get me and my kids a better life. That face I once had such a problem with? It has graced the covers of magazines! Been on billboards across the country, including Times Square, and I won beauty awards. Sometimes, I still have a hard time with the face I see in the mirror if I'm being honest, but for the most part, I shake it off and realize this face is *mine*, not his. I am in control of my life, not him.

I worked a lot, which meant I didn't see my kids nearly as often as I would have liked. I made so many mistakes while trying to do what I could, but I also got us going in the right direction. I had and have an overabundance of love, and I worked on myself enough to provide my children with a mother they remind me often how grateful they are to have. If that were my only accomplishment, I would be fulfilled. To come from what did not feel like love to be able to know what unconditional love is with these kids, what a blessing in itself!

You've read to this point, so some part of this story resonates with you! You see some part of yourself here. Maybe you're in the midst of it. Maybe you're on your way out of it. Sweetheart, it's not easy but it's worth it. Take the first step: look internally at you! The true you. Not the bullshit they try to feed you about who you are and how you should live your life or what is actually happening in your life and to you. Don't let them make you feel crazy or like you're the problem. Accept responsibility for your actions even if you were reacting to theirs. That isn't how you want to show up, I know! So breathe and think before you react.

You will not change others no matter how much you explain yourself, no matter how much you try to control the situation. You have to worry about you! Decide what type of woman you want to be, and start saying no to anything that isn't that. This is a process, and some days you will be a bad bitch, some days you will be a sad bitch, but what you are not going to do is be a lazy bitch! You are going to work hard every day and forgive yourself for when you fuck up, because you will. You are going to follow your heart and the calling God has for you! Then, when the time is right, you are going to share your story with me and we are going to get you in front of those who will resonate with you. And slowly but surely, one by one, together, we are going to change the world for one person at a time. I see you! I love you! You are home! You got this!

That vision I spoke of earlier in this chapter is finally coming together. You see, ever since I was a little girl, I saw myself up on stage in front of many people talking. I also saw myself as an author, a businesswoman, a mom, and a model. I didn't know what it meant at the time but I do now. Today, I am doing all of that, and I am starting to do it on a grander scale. I have finally been able to answer the call from God, the universe, whatever you believe. I answered and here we are. By purchasing this book, you are supporting this vision and this movement to help people know that they are not alone in their circumstances, there is help out there, there is hope, there is a better life waiting around the corner, they just have to take action. There are people from all different backgrounds, political stances, races, creeds, cultures, religious backgrounds, and ages who are part of this movement, and we all love and support each other very much. No one is judging or being hateful. We honor where the other person is coming from and support them with no bias, no competition, just pure love and support. To be seen and heard and respected. What a concept huh?

I am so grateful for your support. I said earlier that you weren't going to be disappointed, and if somehow you've read to this point, I wanna hear from you. You probably have a kick-ass story, and I wanna make you an author! There can NEVER be enough people who want to share their stories and make a difference in the world. Let me help you help me become better together and make an impact on the world!

Therapeutic Summary

In this chapter, Genesis shares her experience of a great deal of trauma, including family violence, neglect, sexual abuse, bullying, and gaslighting. It would be easy to conclude that Genesis could have experienced Post-Traumatic Stress Disorder (PTSD) or Complex PTSD. She mentions anger, "popcorn" memories of her childhood, guilt, shame, and self-harm (cutting and scratching); all of which can be symptoms of PTSD. CPTSD is the result of chronic, long-lasting, or repeated traumatic events during childhood, which results in the still-developing body and brain to continuously be flooded with adrenaline and cortisol, keeping the mind and body in survival mode. It would also be common for people who experience this level of trauma to experience dissociation and/or personality disorders, although that may not have happened in Genesis' situation. While it is never stated, one or both parents in this situation could have experienced their own personality disorder, such as narcissism or borderline personality disorder. The family violence Genesis experienced, specifically by her father, is indicative of narcissistic abuse.

Resources

- Office of Family Violence Prevention and Services — www.acf.hhs.gov
- Center Against Sexual and Family Violence — https://casfv.org
- National Sexual Assault Hotline — www.rainn.org
- The National Foundation to End Child Abuse & Neglect — "What is Complex PTSD?" — www.endcan.org
- The National Child Traumatic Stress Network — www.nctsn.org
- Counseling/Therapy — www.psychologytoday.com

Reflections of Resilience: Seeing Beyond the Surface

GENESIS GOMEZ is an accomplished entrepreneur, 4x number one bestselling author, inspiring public speaker, and supermodel whose mission is to empower individuals to pursue their wildest dreams. Featured in *Forbes* for her five-star professionalism and celebrated in *Fortune Magazine's* prestigious 40 under 40 list, Genesis's achievements are a testament to her dedication and excellence.

As the driving force behind the Reigning Resilient Queens movement, Genesis answered the calling God had for her since she was a little girl and is committed to uplifting women by sharing stories of triumph and resilience. Through this powerful initiative, Genesis has her coaching program called Model Mindset Mastery Services, as well as partners with nonprofits and other organizations focusing on the whole person while embracing beauty inside and out. Genesis believes that doing this is important to a person's overall success. This movement provides tools, guidance, and resources to enhance mental health, financial success, and business growth, helping individuals uncover their true potential.

Genesis's modeling career is adorned with numerous accolades, including wins in spokesmodel competitions, runway, bikini contests, most photogenic, and the title of Ultimate Supermodel 2021. She is proudly signed with the prestigious Donna Baldwin Modeling Agency.

Beyond her professional accomplishments, Genesis is a devoted mother to two beautiful children, who are her greatest source of strength and inspiration. She often reflects on how she wouldn't be where she is today without them.

With Genesis as your coach, you are partnering with someone who embodies resilience and understands the multifaceted challenges and opportunities life presents. She is passionate about helping others look and feel their best while finding purpose and meaning in their lives. Join Genesis Gomez and the Reigning Resilient Queens in celebrating strength, beauty, and the power of sharing our stories.

Keep Up with Genesis

https:/linktr.ee/genesisashleygomez

Photo credits:
billymontanaimages.com
empire.edu/cosmetology-schools/colorado/aurora-denver

Follow our movement:

reigningresilientqueens.com

This Little Light of Mine

Dorie McCleskey

Feeling the sun on my face, and wind in my hair as I race down a dirt trail on my bike, seeing the lizards scurry across the trail as I approach the large rock I love to climb, and I hunt for my next pet to take home for the day. At this moment, I am free and fully alive.

Growing up, I was the happiest person I knew. I felt full of joy as I took on life's journey with open arms and big dreams. I was painfully shy, though you wouldn't know it now. We moved around a lot as a military family, making it difficult to make close friends. The constant change of meeting new people and learning about new places was all very exciting. On a military and mechanics salary, we didn't have much luxury. My two younger brothers and I would play with toy cars for hours, digging tunnels and making trails for them to drive on in the dirt. When visiting my grandmother's house, my cousin and I would play dress-up. I would pretend I owned a real estate company. Dressed in my grandmother's pumps and beads, with stationery and pen in hand, I felt so grown-up. I loved helping her and my mom prepare homes for open houses. It made me feel important to contribute to something so big at such a young age. I have many other fond memories growing up in the small town of Rock Springs, Wyoming.

I am an optimist, almost to a fault. I have given my last penny away more than once, and I would not change a thing. I cherish that every experience has made me who I am today. I have a huge heart for people and I am a people pleaser. I didn't say I was perfect. I'm telling you all this to say that when I gave my all to my second marriage.

My grandmother has always been open about her opinions. Our conversations when I was struggling helped me to see that my light had gone out. It was so difficult to find joy in my life. On the outside, my marriage looked like a perfect fairy tale, with a beautiful home in a nice suburb of Denver, kids in activities to keep us on our toes, and date night scheduled every Friday. Yet, I found myself pondering, *Maybe my husband would be happier if I wasn't around. Maybe I could make it look like an accident by running my car off a cliff or into a tree. Then he could still get my life insurance, and maybe that would make him happy.*

Wait, what? That is crazy thinking!, I told myself. At that moment, I knew I had to do something.

The previous day, I had taken my daughter to the party supply store to get the decorations she wanted for her birthday party. I needed to make a stop to pick up documents from a notary who had done a signing for me but was not going to be able to get them to the title company on time. I had given my husband access to my location through a map app so that he could locate me in case of an emergency. When he saw that I was not where he expected me to be, he called demanding to know what I was doing twenty minutes away and not at the party store as expected. His brother had just arrived at our home to make a very involved birthday cake with our daughter. When I told him that I had already been to that party store and why I was picking up the documents, he became furious. The cake they wanted to make was going to take some time, so I could understand the stress of not having our daughter at home when his brother got there. Only, he had never set a specific time with me. What my husband seemed most angry about was that I was out doing business. I had never felt so embarrassed and angry in my life. He was shaming me for something that wasn't even wrong or immoral, in front of our daughter. The worst feeling came when we got home. He acted as though nothing had happened. *Who is this man?* This was the straw that broke the camel's back. I knew then that I was not going to tolerate the relationship this way.

After telling me that he hated my career because it took his wife away from him, I did everything I could to slow my work pace. He was afraid I would become like his brother and cheat on him. This was a huge blow to me. What I had created in my loan signing company made me feel valued and important. I was working hard to create something we could both be proud of, and I had proven to myself that I could create a successful business. My husband had become accustomed to me running a preschool and childcare from our home for the previous eleven years. I would cook and clean and, of course, take care of our children. Though I had his buy-in to support me in my new career, it made sense that the change was very taxing on him and the family.

He would constantly pine for my time. Seeing his pain, I asked my husband to create gratitudes with me in the morning so that we could focus on the good in our life and spend time together every morning. We also started doing yoga together and would go on the occasional bike ride. Yet there was still something missing. He wasn't taking me on trips anymore. He would say that if I wanted to go, I would need to save up for the trip. This was not an easy thing for me. I had just started the signing company the year before, in 2020. Although it did very well in this previous year, refinances were dwindling, and I needed to focus on the debt that was building up as the industry came to a screeching halt. I was taking every signing I could to ensure the business would still make it through the real estate decline. This appeared to make my husband very angry. At the time, he didn't understand that it takes time to build a business.

One of my husband's complaints was that I am a terrible communicator. So, I enrolled in a personal and professional development training to improve my communication skills. The forum I attended reminded me of a seminar at my son's boarding school in Utah. Like the seminar, the forum gave me tools that would build upon my self-worth and transform my way of being in life. I had placed my value in what others thought of me. I have always been a "yes girl," doing whatever was asked of me. What was missing was what *I* wanted for my life. The counselor at my son's school suggested a book about codependency. I had no idea what that was, but figured if she suggested it, then it must be important to my son's development. What I discovered was that the book was about me. I am codependent. This way of being is what has formed the relationship with my husband. It wasn't healthy. Of course, being the fixer that I am, I had to try harder.

I asked my husband to join a session so he could see what I was learning, and perhaps he would like to work on it with me. I thought it could make a huge difference in our communication and improve our relationship. He said he would check it out. At the last minute, he was a no-show. When I asked why he didn't attend, he said he didn't want to be pressured into spending money. I am not sure what that was about, but I could guess it had something to do with how poor he grew up. His biggest trigger has always been around money. Nonetheless, I was very disappointed. Someone who put such a big emphasis on our relationship would not put any resources into himself to better our relationship. When I asked if there was room in the budget for me to see a counselor, my husband asked if I was leaving him. My response was that I was extremely depressed and I needed support. Thinking it was odd that he asked if I was leaving made me think that maybe he was miserable in the marriage too.

My husband always said he was supportive of my career, but his actions and constant requests for me to give up my business said otherwise. When I started my signing company, I specifically stated to him that it is a boundary I am holding for myself. I was not giving it up upon his request as I did with everything else he was not pleased with me doing. When I ran my childcare, I would have activities to get out of the house a few times a week. There were several MLM ventures, kung fu to make time for my kids, women's bible study, etc. Eventually, I would get tired of battling his complaints, only to lose out on something else I enjoyed. Yes, I had been late to the occasional date night and requested that some were spent at home cuddling on the couch, especially when I was exhausted from a very busy week. Not being home to make dinner every evening, my mom would step in to help because my husband didn't want to cook. He started to ask a friend over on our date nights. Knowing I would be home late, I agreed. I wanted him to have friends he could spend his time with. That is what makes a healthy relationship, right?

A conversation with one of my husband's friends took me by surprise. He said my husband always speaks so highly of me. I was surprised because the feeling I got from him was that I was never enough. Every time I thought I met an expectation, the bar was raised higher or there was another hoop to jump through, another expectation to meet. Sometimes, it was someone else in the equation, like my son from a previous marriage, or my mother, who he requested to move into her own home so we could work on our marriage. When I confronted my husband about how he made me feel, he said: "You have to want to change." *What the eff!?* Without skipping a beat, I replied, "That's just it, Dear Husband. I like who I am!"

Our dance kept building until we were back at square one. He decided we were not reserving Friday for date night anymore because I wasn't home before six o'clock p.m. most evenings anyway. I knew we were growing apart when he planned several trips out of state without me. His reasoning was that I would probably have trouble because of my rheumatoid arthritis or that I didn't have funds to go on the trip he planned to take our youngest daughter on. I had given him every penny that my business brought in for the entirety of our marriage. I would reserve small amounts for things I wanted but was questioned about everything I bought. He felt like I was holding out on him when I didn't have the funds from my business to pay for what I previously had when running my childcare business. I was trying to keep my business afloat and clearly communicated this to him.

When we bought our home years prior, he was making half as much income as he was at this point. Somehow, his now six-figure income couldn't allow for me to have space and time to learn from what was happening in my business? According to his calculations, he needed me to bring in half the money since I was spending so much time on my business. This was one justification for asking me to close my business. He became relentless in asking.

The day he demanded it more than a few times was the day I called the lawyer. Spent beyond measure, I had discovered that I was no longer in love with him. I hated the way I felt just being around him. I want my light to shine again! Through the coaching and training I received and creating who I decided to be every day, I started to see that light again.

When I sat my husband down to speak with him about filing for divorce, he burst into tears. I had only seen him cry a handful of times at the most. I thought he would have expected this after the comments he made and the communications we were having. He thought we were getting better because of the daily gratitudes and yoga. He asked if there was someone else. When I replied, "No," he said it would have been easier on him if there was. He couldn't fathom that I would just leave because I wasn't happy in our relationship. I soon started seeing a very vindictive side of him that I didn't know was there. We would argue back and forth, blaming each other for what we weren't getting out of the relationship.

Being in the personal development program, I had the opportunity to work with a coach. One of the sessions with her led to me complaining about a trip he went on without me while he was still complaining about me spending money. My coach asked me something profound. She said, "I wonder what this divorce has been like for him?"

What? I was confused. *Why would I care?* She helped me to discover that I was spending so much energy on blaming him and victimizing myself, I couldn't hear anything he was saying, and we were not getting anywhere in our conversations. I thought I had it all figured out and knew what his response would be to anything I said or did. She suggested I listen to him from a space where nothing's wrong, ask him what this divorce has been like for him, and really listen to what he was saying. This wasn't something I wanted to do, but I decided to do it anyway. *What could it hurt?* We weren't getting anywhere at the pace we were going.

Magical! In allowing him to be heard, he was able to express everything he was experiencing without interruption. He then asked if I wanted the same opportunity. In hindsight, I can see that even listening in a space where I felt he was blaming me, had me trying to fix the problem. Sometimes, there is nothing to fix—there is only someone wanting to be heard. This exercise made me feel as though I had power over myself and the situation again.

After this conversation, we decided that we would be the best co-parents the world has ever seen. Our mediation, according to the lawyers, was the most peaceful meditation they had ever experienced. They were surprised at the ease in which we agreed upon the terms of the divorce. The money portion took a little longer in the negotiation. Neither of us got exactly what we wanted and neither of us seemed to feel taken advantage of either. I made the difficult decision to close my signing company as the debt from not being active in doing signings created an even bigger debt that I didn't see myself coming out of. Everything else moved quickly. Between my husband and myself, we had already spent around twenty grand on a peaceful divorce. I don't want to imagine what it would have looked like had we not had the conversation we had that evening.

My soon-to-be-former husband suggested that he buy me out of the house, so I could find something in my price range. To refinance our current home, I would need to take out a second mortgage. He didn't want me to be house poor and possibly lose the house. We were working hard to keep our two girls in it so they could have some stability in this already difficult situation they were thrown into. This was exciting! I could start new, like I had envisioned during a coaching session with a dear friend. She took me through a powerful visualization of picturing my new home and life. I wasn't sure how it would happen, but I was excited for the future I envisioned.

At the time, one of my husband's brothers was being transferred out of state. Knowing their home was in my price range, I made a bold request to purchase it. I had been looking at homes and watching them fly off the market at several thousand more than the asking price. To my surprise, they accepted my request. We were still waiting for the divorce to be finalized, and I had to wait for the refinance of our current home. I had to move quickly, and luckily, I had a friend already working on my loan.

I was in awe as everything was lining up so perfectly. I became the proud owner of a beautiful ranch-style home with gray cobblestone trim. It had a decent-sized backyard for my girls to play in, and I had no worries about the conditions of the home as I knew it had been well cared for. When I did a Zoom video to share the news and show my home to my friend, who coached me through the visualization, I realized it was the home I had visualized several months prior. This was amazing!!! It encouraged me about everything else I had envisioned for my life.

There is so much still happening around me. The last few years following the divorce have been challenging. The grief from the loss of the relationship that could have been was almost too much to bear. My little light has had some very dim and dark moments. However, my tenacious spirit refuses to give up hope. Every day is an opportunity for a new beginning, and my light is shining brighter and brighter.

Therapeutic Summary

Dorie was struggling with codependency, which led to depression and suicidal ideation at one point. People pleasing is a key characteristic of codependency, as is a lack of boundaries. It is not uncommon for people who have codependent personalities to experience depression and or anxiety. It also has a huge impact on your relationships and how you function in those relationships.

The inability to say no and to try to make everyone around you happy at your expense will ultimately take its toll physically and mentally, as Dorie described here.

Resources

- Codependents Anonymous — coda.org
- National Suicide Prevention Hotline — 800-273-TALK (8255) or 988lifeline.org
- Counselors/Therapists — psychologytoday.com

DORIE MCCLESKEY is a big dreamer. As an entrepreneurial team player who quickly identifies opportunities and adjusts accordingly, she has taken on several business ventures throughout her life.

A respected leader in her local community known for inspiring others, fostering credibility, empowering teams and motivating staff to excellence with the outcome of producing extraordinary results.

Her greatest joys are her four delightful children, each beautifully unique in their personalities and abilities. She has a genuine love for people and enjoys hiking, yoga, and playing with puppies.

Her welcoming demeanor, love of learning, and engaging in personal conversations fuel her ability to be inquisitive and observant with everyone she encounters.

Keep Up with Dorie

http://Linktr.ee/toDorie

Photo credits:
d20photography.com
empire.edu/cosmetology-schools/colorado/aurora-denver

Follow our movement:

reigningresilientqueens.com

Self-Love

Gabby Gonzalez

"The number on the scale does not define your worth" is what my therapists would always tell me. I thought they were all crazy. Of course it did! The world would treat me differently depending on what the scale said, so every morning, immediately after waking up, I would weigh myself to gauge my worth and self-esteem for that day.

I've struggled with body dysmorphia and overeating since I was a small child. Kids in school would bully me, calling me ogre (which rhymed with Olga, my legal name at the time), fat, disgusting, ugly, and the list goes on. My family would compare me to the skinnier siblings or cousins and would comment on my weight whenever I walked into the room. At one point, I got to 230 pounds, and I remember being so big I was reluctant to go to my 8th-grade continuation because I was ashamed of what I looked like in a dress.

The adults put me on various diets, and many times, I had to eat a different meal than everyone else at the table to abide by whatever rules and restrictions were set for me on that day. The spotlight on my weight became the root of my obsession with how I thought the world perceived me. I was convinced at an early age that because of how my body looked, I was not deserving of love or existence. I became committed to making myself invisible by taking up less space, ensuring that I didn't get in anyone's way. And I did just that, this 230-pound ten-year-old became a 139-pound fourteen-year-old, all thanks to restrictive eating, an obsession with exercising, and purging. I got thin, and the world started to respect and praise me for how I looked. "Keep doing what you are doing" is what I heard often from the people around me.

That motivated me to keep up the lifestyle and take it to the extreme, eventually developing bulimia and binge-eating disorders. I became obsessed with finding the most effective diet or diet pill, but none provided a permanent solution. Once I got off the diet or the pills, I would gain weight again and the cycle would start over. By age twenty-seven, I finally had enough money to pay for a $20,000 cosmetic surgery procedure I had dreamed of since I was a little girl.

I had an abdominoplasty to remove the extra skin I had permanently developed due to the excess amount of weight I had as a child. I also opted for a boob job and liposuction. This procedure is what is known as a "mommy makeover," except I had never given birth to a child, which was embarrassing, to say the least.

The recovery was brutal and lasted more than six months. It took me weeks before I could muster the courage to look at myself in the mirror. I had a heavy anxiety about being in this new body and seeing the scars, stitches, and wounds all over. Why did I go through all this pain? Well, I thought for sure that this massive body change would solidify my worth, and I would finally feel adequate and get the love and respect I had so desperately been seeking.

But surprise! It didn't change anything. In fact, my body dysmorphia went to a whole new level. I felt so defeated and could not understand why nothing worked. I was left with no option but to look within myself to uncover the root of the behaviors and mistreatment I had been inflicting on myself. The healing needed to start from within, demanding a raw, unfiltered deconstruction of my past.

"The number on the scale does not define your worth." After months of eating-disorder therapy and support groups, along with working with a nutritionist, a shift started to happen. I questioned my beliefs. *Does my body really define whether I deserve to be loved or not? Where does the root of my hate toward myself come from?* My therapist had me dig further, and I took a deep dive into my childhood. I realized I had a burning hatred and embarrassment for that little girl from the past. I truly believed that it was all her fault that others didn't respect us. I would think, *If you weren't so fat and ugly, we wouldn't have suffered or been neglected by the family or by the world.* I had no sympathy for that little girl. I thought she betrayed both of us with her lazy and gluttonous behaviors.

Over time, I was able to come to another realization, that this child was just that ... a child! She was doing her very best with the information, knowledge, and resources that she had at the time. Food was a way to cope with the lack of support and love that she was not receiving from the adults who were around.

I uncovered that the resentment I had toward my childhood self stemmed from the messages I was receiving from the world at a young age. I identified with those ideas and beliefs and made them my own. The therapist and members of my eating disorder support groups gave me the courage to question those beliefs and create new ones for myself.

I realized that allowing self-hatred to live within me was just continuing to give power to the adults that I had been carrying a resentment against for all these years. I had been waiting for an apology that I was never going to get, and it was finally time for me to take back the power by learning to love all parts of me, including the little girl that others didn't know how to love. This is something I work on daily. The stories about my past still come up unexpectedly, but they are much quieter now. The awareness has given me the ability to make a better choice, the choice to speak to myself and of myself with the utmost respect and love that I deserve. Nobody can define what I am worth except me, and I know now that I am neither below nor above my fellow human. We are all God's children, created in His perfect image, and nobody is made by mistake.

ADDICTION

I met D on January 19th, 2017, at my best friend Ben's birthday party. I had known Ben for four years by this point and never heard of D until the week leading up to the party. Ben and D had reconnected on Facebook, they met up for lunch. D asked Ben about the girl who was tagged all over his Facebook. Ben let him know about me and told D, "You will never get with her." That didn't stop D. He came over to Ben's house before the party while we were getting ready, brought a six-pack of craft beer, and we hit it off right away. By the end of the night, D had put his number in my phone and kissed me good night. I told him to text me when he got home to make sure he was safe, and he did.

From that day forward, we were inseparable. We texted or talked every day. Soon after we went on our first date, D came to pick me up in his cute black Mazda RX8 stick shift with a red leather interior, which was right up my alley. He drove us to what became our favorite sushi spot, and the date was unforgettable.

By date number three, I remembered looking at D from across the table over pizza and beer, and I knew at that very moment I was going to marry this man. We made our relationship official on February 8th, got engaged in April, and eloped on July 18th, 2017. I moved in with him quickly after we met and purchased his grandmother's home for us to live in by November 2017. I felt like this was the man that I was going to take on the world with and that it would truly be "till death do us part." Everyone thought we were crazy, and that getting married this quickly was a complete mistake. We didn't care, and at the time, I was determined to prove everyone wrong.

Seems like a fairy tale story built on passionate love and infatuation, right? Unfortunately, the truth was our relationship was also built on alcohol and lies. D and I drank *a lot*. We centered many of our activities around drinking. We both had a love for beer, which seemed like another great hobby we had in common. And you know what does not mix well with alcohol? Trauma, pain, and baggage, which we both equally brought with us into the relationship. This created a recipe for chaos and destruction in our home.

There were holes in the wall, busted cell phones, household items from being thrown, doors in the house that I had torn down, and a terrified dog that would hide in the bedroom shaking in fear from all the loud noise and yelling. Over time, I realized that something was very wrong. D was constantly saying that I was the problem, so I started to cut down on drinking.

As I began to sober up, I noticed odd behaviors that D was displaying. It started with him not wanting to sleep with me on our first wedding anniversary. I remember that day so clearly. I was extremely heartbroken, experiencing physical pain in my heart from the rejection and the intense feeling of inadequacy. This behavior escalated to him not being able to look me in the eyes whenever we would get intimate. I would have dinner made, and he would call me at the last minute to tell me that he wouldn't be able to make it home in time for dinner for one reason or another.

Bills wouldn't get paid. He would stop picking up the phone when I called him, and he wouldn't respond to my text messages. This eventually turned into him not coming home on the weekends. I would call his family or friends frantically to see if they knew where he was and if he was okay. I spent many sleepless nights waiting for him to come home, praying to God that he was not in a car accident or dead. It was complete emotional torture for me.

Whenever I would bring up issues, he would say I was acting crazy and that I was the one in the wrong. I started to believe him, and to be completely honest, looking back, I *was* acting crazy. I would blow up his phone with back-to-back calls, drive around to look for him, trying anything to figure out his location. I thought for sure this man was cheating on me or using drugs or both.

I didn't know how to deal with this, so I would also act out and find ways to cope with the emotional rollercoaster I was on. I would go to the neighborhood bars on my own, hang out with other men, or go out with friends to distract myself. Our life was in complete chaos.

On the morning of September 29th, 2019, D finally admitted he had been using drugs since December 2017. The funny thing was, I already knew deep down he had been using drugs all these years. Again and again, I would ask him all the time if he was on drugs, and he would dismiss it. I recognized all the signs after having been around it since I was fourteen years old, growing up as a drug user myself, but I also so desperately wanted to believe him every time he would tell me he wasn't using drugs. I was living in complete denial. Even after finding out about his addiction, I tried to find others to blame or lash out at for D using drugs. I blamed his dealer, our family members who partook in getting high with him, and even blamed his mom for not telling me she knew about his drug use before I found out. I wanted someone else to be responsible for this.

It took a long time for D to get help, and an even longer time for me to accept that I could not be the one to rescue him from the drugs. The majority of my twenties revolved around trying to "save" D and keep him clean. I gave him ultimatums and forced him into marriage counseling, therapy, and recovery meetings. I would keep tabs on how many meetings he went to and how often. I smelled his breath and checked his eyes when he walked through the door. All this attention to detail and my obsession with controlling his recovery, and yet, D kept relapsing.

I kicked him out multiple times for showing up high to see me. I even divorced the man, and it didn't keep him clean. I went from acting crazy for not knowing if he was using drugs to acting crazy trying to keep him off the drugs. In my heart, I believed that if I did not try to keep him clean, he would die from an overdose or accident, and it would be my fault that I let it happen.

The worst part is that I was going through most of this by myself. I kept this a secret as much as I could. Because I felt so much shame for staying in the relationship, I didn't want anyone to know the severity of what I was dealing with. I couldn't understand why it was so difficult for me to leave the relationship even though it was ruining my life. Daily, I would pray to whoever was out there to give me the courage and wisdom to get me out of this situation.

One day, I ended up sharing my story with the new gal at work. It turned out that she had dealt with a similar situation with her son's father. This woman, who ended up becoming a dear friend of mine, gave me information about a support group for families of addicted loved ones. I took the information and connected with the group soon after our conversation.

Within the group, I met others from all walks of life who were dealing with the same struggles that I was going through with D. I was not alone in this, which was a huge relief because, for so long, I had felt completely alone.

It turns out that addiction does not discriminate. It affects all genders, races, socioeconomic backgrounds, and ages. There were parents, siblings, spouses, and children on the other side of the addiction, and we were all just trying to save our loved ones from the drugs. What I learned was that I have no power over the disease of addiction or my loved one who was addicted to drugs and alcohol. Through the stories I heard and the internal work that I did, I realized that D was addicted to drugs, and I was addicted to keeping him clean because I wanted to get back the man I had married before the drugs. I also started to recognize how I was participating in the chaos of the relationship. I was making D responsible for my happiness, self-worth, and peace instead of taking ownership of my own life. I was also using D's addiction as an excuse for me not to change. It was easy to point the finger at him for all my suffering since he was the one visibly making the mistakes. I would make myself seem like the victim in the relationship. I was seeking the attention and sympathy of others by telling them my version of the story and then using that sympathy to keep myself distracted from having to change my behaviors.

I was as guilty as D was. I actively contributed to the chaos, lies, and destruction of the relationship. I lied, cheated, and manipulated throughout the relationship to cope with my pain. And while there were moments when we brought out the best in each other, we also brought out the absolute worst. True love sometimes means sacrificing your own desires for the sake of someone else's growth and well-being. I came to the harsh realization that D was never going to recover and stay clean with me in his life—a truth that I still struggle to fully grasp today.

Forgiveness and Gratitude

Recovering and healing is messy. It is difficult. It is painful. Recovering and healing is also rewarding and liberating. As I look back at some of the most difficult parts of my life, I know for a fact that any type of healing requires forgiveness. According to the Mayo Clinic, forgiveness involves an intentional decision to let go of anger and resentment.

It began with forgiving myself—for the mistakes I made that caused pain to both myself and my loved ones. I forgave myself for believing that D chose drugs over our family because I was not worthy enough or beautiful enough as a woman. I had to let go of my regret for turning my back on God and for desperately clinging on to a relationship with D for far too long.

I learned that I wasn't ready to move on until I was truly prepared to do so, and I had to give myself permission to be loving and patient toward myself along the way. I asked God daily to change my heart. This process of self-forgiveness made it possible for me to forgive others and, most importantly, to forgive God.

Over the years, I also made amends with several loved ones. I've made many mistakes along the way, and it's crucial to make things right where I've wronged people because regrets only weigh down my spirit if left unresolved.

Forgiving doesn't mean erasing the past or expecting others to forget the wrongs done to them, but it does allow me to move forward without carrying the heavy burden of past pain.

I forgave that little girl and am continuing to find forgiveness for the people who spoke unkindly to her. I forgave my ex-husband. For a time, I believed that getting together with D was the biggest mistake I had made in my life and that I had wasted all my twenties on a relationship with this man. I have now changed that story, and today, I am filled with an immense amount of gratitude for that experience. My relationship with D was a gift, and he has been an impactful teacher to me—a guide, an angel. Now, I pray for him from a place of love and hope, supporting his journey from a distance.

Forgiveness is the only way to make room for what God has planned next. The door to the past must be closed for the door to the next season to open. It is time to move forward. We can do hard things.

> "I can do all things through Christ who strengthens me." —Philippians 4:13

Therapeutic Summary

In this chapter, we see Gabby dealing with body dysmorphia, an eating disorder (bulimia specifically), reported substance use as a teen, her husband's substance abuse and addiction, and the signs of codependency. Codependency is common amongst spouses and family members of addicts and people with severe mental health issues. Gabby describes the codependency perfectly when she writes, "I also started to recognize how I was participating in the chaos of the relationship…"

Resources

- Al-Anon Support Group for Families of Addicts — al-anon.org
- Celebrate Recovery Christian Program for Addiction, Families of Addicts & Mental Health Issues -celebraterecovery.com
- Codependency Counseling — heatherbrookelpc.com and psychologytoday.com
- Eating Recovery Foundation for inpatient/outpatient care eatingrecoverycenter.com
- Narcotics Anonymous na.org
- NAR Anon nar-anon.org
- National Eating Disorders Association — nationaleatingdisorders.org

Gabriela Xiomara Gonzalez is a dynamic public speaker and full-time educator, committed to empowering others through her remarkable personal journey and dedication to service. As a first-generation Mexican American and the daughter of immigrant parents, she embraced the values of hard work and perseverance early on, which have helped her navigate and overcome various life challenges.

Gabby has seen the profound impact that accountability, self-worth, vulnerability, and faith can have on personal transformation. She is passionate about sharing these insights through her speaking engagements, focusing on mental health, generational healing, self-worth, and the crucial role of taking ownership of one's own healing and growth.

Keep Up with Gabby

https://linktr.ee/gxgspeaks

Photo credits:
d20photography.com
empire.edu/cosmetology-schools/colorado/aurora-denver

Follow our movement:

reigningresilientqueens.com

A Journey from Heart Bondage to Freedom

Heather Brooke

THERE I WAS SITTING on the cold tile floor with photo albums scattered around me and tears rolling down my face. I was six years old and had just read a handwritten poem in my parent's wedding album. My mom loved reading and writing poetry. To this day, I don't know if she wrote that poem or if she had simply copied it; but what I do know is that the enemy (Satan) took that opportunity to place a heart bondage on me that I would operate out of for the next thirty-plus years.

You see, the poem was about a woman finding out she was pregnant with a daughter and her husband being upset because he wanted a son. My six-year-old, undeveloped brain took on the message, "My father didn't want me and doesn't love me."

When asked how I'd describe my upbringing, I would say I grew up in an average, upper-middle-class family. Both of my parents had careers. My mom was a radiology technician, and my dad was a general contractor and railroad engineer. My brother (who's two years younger) and I were good friends growing up. We played every sport imaginable, and I excelled as a fast-pitch softball pitcher until I quit in high school. Our parents coached our sports teams. When they weren't coaching, they were still at our practices and games. My parents' relationship had plenty of ups, downs, and arguments; however, I remember us being a pretty close family until I was ten or eleven.

Around ten years old was when life really changed for me. The enemy had placed the heart bondage on me a few years earlier, but to this point, it hadn't really impacted me. That changed when I began being groomed and molested by an older cousin. I was full of shame, fear, anxiety, and self-hate.

While my parents were well meaning, they were not always emotionally available. It had been drilled into me to talk about it if anyone ever did anything to me, but I didn't trust my dad's anger enough to tell my parents what my cousin was doing to me. I believed that if I told, my dad's temper would lead to him being in prison, so I kept it internalized. That internalization manifested itself in a hair-pulling disorder called trichotillomania.

Much like an alcoholic with their first drink or a drug addict with their first hit, I remember that first pull vividly. My eye was burning, so I walked to the mirror in our hallway and noticed an eyelash curled under. I began pulling at the lash with my nails, attempting to straighten it out, when all of a sudden, the lash came out of my eyelid, and for a split second, all the tension and anxiety that had been building and holding in my body washed away. The only way I can describe it is that the pull is similar to someone who cuts themselves and gets that initial release from the pain of the cut. It was a moment of relief and release, followed by even more shame and guilt than I had felt before. It kept me stuck in a negative cycle of anxiety, release, shame, guilt, anxiety, release, shame, guilt—and on it went.

I had the disorder for a while before my grandmother, who noticed my missing lashes, asked what happened. My response was to lie. It was the early 90s, and we didn't have the Internet, so I had no way of knowing at the time that what I was doing was a disorder, that it had a name, or that other people did it. I felt alone. I felt shame. I felt like a freak. *Who pulls out their hair? What's wrong with you? Why can't you just stop? You're a freak. You're broken. Something's wrong with you.*

These were questions and statements I asked myself regularly. In an attempt to stop pulling my lashes, I made the conscious rationalization that if I started pulling from somewhere else, I could control that pulling and stop pulling my lashes. My rationale was illogical, and before long, my Brooke Shields eyebrows were nonexistent as well as my lashes, and I was waking up to piles of hair on my bedroom floor next to my bed.

At this point, I was pulling both consciously and subconsciously, and my self-esteem, self-worth, and self-love were tanking. I grew up watching Miss Texas and Miss America on television and had dreamed of being on those stages one day. How was I ever going to reach my dreams if I didn't have eyelashes, eyebrows, or hair? I also wondered, *How would I ever get a boyfriend or get married? Who could love someone who pulled out their own hair? Why can't I stop?*

I was going into my sophomore year in high school when I found out through a late-night infomercial that other people pulled their hair and that it had a name: trichotillomania. I sat with tears rolling down my face, feeling both relief and sadness as the woman on the television gave my disorder a name, but stated there was no cure or treatment for it. A couple of days later, when my mom noticed the bald patches through my thinning, wet ponytail while getting out of our pool, I told her what I had heard on the television.

She scheduled an appointment for me to see a doctor she worked for. He officially gave me a diagnosis, put me on an antidepressant, and sent me to a psychiatrist an hour away from our home. The antidepressant made it hard for me to function during the day, especially at school, and I began failing some classes. The psychiatrist didn't bother getting any background history on me, and just tried to manage the pulling rather than attempting to find out what triggered it. After a couple of months and no progress, my parents stopped taking me to see the psychiatrist, and I went back to trying to manage it on my own.

By my junior year, I was wearing eyeliner to cover up the missing lashes, penciling in my eyebrows, and wearing a wig to cover the bald patches on my head. I had gone to church youth group all through middle school and high school and prayed every night for God to take this horrible disorder away from me.

While I didn't get bullied at school, I got bullied at home. My brother would say things to me like, "Why can't you just be normal?" My dad would try to embarrass me out of pulling in front of people, and would ground me and punish me when I pulled. By today's standards, if anyone had known, he would've been accused of abuse. And while my mom tried to be more understanding, she never challenged my dad's behavior or punishments.

Don't get me wrong, my parents are good people, but they weren't emotionally intelligent enough at the time to deal with my issues in an appropriate way. And because I was already getting in trouble for something I couldn't control, I decided I might as well do things worth getting in trouble over. After a couple of boys broke up with me for not having sex with them, I became promiscuous, believing that was the only way I was ever going to get someone to love me, adding to the negative messages and the heart bondage from ten years prior.

While I was attending church, had been saved in 8th grade and was baptized in 10th, I wasn't living the life of a follower of Christ. I'd go to youth on Wednesday night, go to church on Sunday morning, and then go back Sunday evening for discipleship, youth choir, and Sunday evening service. But when church was over on Sunday, I'd hit dirt roads to drink and smoke with my friends. I'd go to parties on Friday and Saturday nights and drink and smoke cigarettes on our lunch break during school. I kept a water bottle of vodka in my locker and would sneak out of the house with whoever my boyfriend was at the time. I believed in God, but I was angry with him and believed he loved everyone except me.

Fast-forward through ten more years of trauma. I finally ended up earning my master's degree in Clinical Mental Health Counseling in 2012.

Around this same time, is when I started talking publicly and openly about my trichotillomania, making my first conversation about the disorder through a blog and a Facebook post. That was the scariest thing I had ever done. I was preparing for name-calling, for questions, for rejection. But what I got instead was empathy, support, encouragement, and people who I had known for years sharing their stories of either experiencing trichotillomania themselves or knowing someone else who had it. That was the first time I had felt free from hiding it for over twenty years.

In 2017, I was encouraged to compete in the Ms. Woman Colorado United States Pageant, using trichotillomania as my platform, and I won. This resulted in my partnership with Hair Club and appearing in their commercials, print advertising, and being named a brand ambassador, a partnership I still have with them today. Ms. Woman Colorado gave me the opportunity to talk more about my disorder, and because of this, professionally, I began treating clients with trichotillomania at the clinic where I was working. I had been pulling for over twenty-five years at this point, still praying for God to take it away, and wavering back and forth in my relationship with Him, wanting to believe He could heal me, but also doubting He cared enough to do it.

In 2018, a woman brought in her fourteen-year-old stepdaughter at the recommendation of their occupational therapist, who had told the woman the child had trichotillomania and gave them a lot of inaccurate information about the disorder. The girl was on the autism spectrum and was nonverbal. When trying to connect with youth, I enjoyed using books they could relate to. This was the young girl I had worked with who had trichotillomania, so I went to the Internet looking for a book to share with her. I found books for therapists, parents, and adults with trichotillomania; but nothing at all for teens. I sat at my desk after that session and, in ten minutes, loosely using my story, wrote a book for children and sent it to my mom, who illustrated the book.

Later that year, I self-published *Where's My Hair? A Trichotillomania Story for Children* and won Children's Author of 2023 from the InspireU Network. After publishing the book, I began getting messages from people all over the world thanking me for writing the book, including adults saying they wished they had my book when they were children. It was after publishing my book that I realized that God had not forsaken me. He was using what I had gone through to help other people.

Now, I want to go back for just a minute because I started this chapter talking about a heart bondage that I was still operating out of up until nine months ago. So, going back to 2018, when I published my book, I think it's important to note that was when I began my deliverance journey and my relationship with Christ really started. For the past year and a half, I had been in an abusive relationship with a narcissist, due to the codependency I was experiencing between how I was raised, my low self-esteem due to my trichotillomania, and the heart bondage that had been placed on me all those years earlier. Leaving the narcissist in 2018 wasn't just a physical and emotional battle, it was spiritual warfare. After a thirty-day-long migraine that sent me to the emergency room a couple of times, resulted in MRIs, a month of doctor visits with every doctor imaginable, and seizures (which I'd never experienced previously), I realized I was fighting a spiritual battle, not a physical one.

One night, I knew I had to have no contact with this man, but I had been struggling to do so. I ran myself a bubble bath, lit candles, and climbed into the tub with my phone like I had been doing every night for almost that entire month. My nightly self-care was a bath and an Elevation Church sermon immediately before bed. This night was different. I had been in so much pain. I was exhausted physically, mentally, and emotionally. I began playing the sermon and felt God talking to me the entire time. I sat in the tub bawling. When the pastor gave the altar call to accept Christ at the end of his sermon, I rededicated my life to Him and baptized myself in my bathtub right then. I slid under the water and bubbles and came back up, repeating this two more times for good measure (in the name of the Father, the Son and the Holy Spirit). When I came up the third time, I grabbed my phone and immediately blocked my ex on absolutely everything. For the first time in months, I had enough strength to do something I'd been struggling so hard with. I then got out of the tub and went to bed. When I woke up the next morning, the migraine was half the pain level it had been. By the next day, it was gone. That was the first time I can really recall God being with me and feeling like He loved and cared about me.

Fast-forward to the present. After spending a few years working on my codependency issues, getting closer to God, and serving in my church, I met an amazing man in acting class, who was also a Christian. We dated for a few months before he moved to Tennessee for a new contract job. When that job became permanent, my youngest daughter and I moved out to Tennessee to be with him.

I reluctantly gave up the house that had been my home for the past three years and the only place that had felt like a home for me and my girls ever. I left my successful private practice in Colorado. I left my friends and family. The hardest of all was leaving my church. I didn't believe I'd find a church that I would connect with the way I did this one.

I began researching churches close to where we would be moving, but before I could check out any of them, my partner found a church and took me there on a visit. Other than having attended a live church service at Elevation Church in Charlotte on a spring break trip with my kids, I had never stepped into a church where I immediately felt the presence of the Lord. But the minute we walked into Love and Truth, there was no doubt that God's presence was there. By the time the sermon was over, I knew I had found my new church home.

Over the next couple of months, I joined a women's group, called The Freedom Class, led by Debbie Wallace. Debbie is the author of the book *Instead of Shame*. This book opened my eyes to the heart bondage that had been placed on me as a child and showed me how I had been unknowingly living out that heart bondage through all my responses to the things that had happened to me.

The class taught me I had facts about my life that I couldn't change, but the facts and God's truth about those facts were two different things. The class, which spanned almost a year, helped me learn how to put on the full armor of God, fight my battles spiritually, and, most importantly, fully and wholeheartedly trust God with everything. This last part has continued to be a process, but I'm learning when He tells me to move, I move. When He tells me to wait, I wait. I am learning to give up my need to control things and the outcome, and to trust that God's will is going to be better than anything I can ask for or want. That being said, a couple of weeks ago, I met with Ms. Debbie and decided to fully rededicate my life to Christ in front of the church, and was officially baptized as a more spiritually mature Christian and adult.

God has shown me, personally and professionally, that He keeps His promises. Anything the enemy means for evil, God will turn to good. That's exactly what He has done with my pain. He's using me and my pain to help others heal emotionally and spiritually. He may not have taken away my trichotillomania, but I no longer see it as something that is a negative thing in my life. God gave my pain purpose, and He will give yours purpose too.

Heavenly Father, I pray for the person reading this chapter and this book. I pray that they find hope, inspiration, and encouragement in these words. I rebuke any feelings of isolation, loneliness, fear, anxiety, depression, addiction, and any other struggles from their life. I pray for peace, joy, love, and freedom that only you can provide for each and every person reading this. I pray, Lord, that you will touch their life. And if they don't already know you, Lord, I pray that you will touch their hearts and give them the desire to know you intimately and experience firsthand the peace and love that you've allowed me to experience, that only you can provide, and that surpasses all our understanding. In Jesus' Holy Name, I pray. Amen.

Therapeutic Summary

In this chapter, I struggled with a heart bondage, sexual abuse, trichotillomania and codependency.

Heart bondage is a combination of a spiritual and mental health issue, so I would encourage you to explore this particular issue by reading *Instead of Shame* by Debbie Wallace, if you believe you are dealing with anything in this area.

In this specific case, my trichotillomania developed as a result of the trauma I experienced and as a way of dealing with the anxiety that I was experiencing.

Addressing childhood sexual trauma, the earlier treatment is sought, the better. There are therapists trained specifically in trauma and childhood trauma. Trauma can result in what we call comorbidity, which means that as a result of the trauma, you have more than one mental health diagnosis. In my case, trichotillomania and anxiety. Trauma specialists can address the trauma, as well as the diagnosed conditions related to the trauma.

Trichotillomania has no cure at this time; however, cognitive behavioral therapy and dietary changes and supplements have been shown to be helpful to some people.

Codependency can result as a symptom of trauma, emotionally unavailable caregivers and/or caregivers with their own severe mental health or substance abuse issues. Codependency looks like people pleasing, putting others before yourself, self-doubt, low self-esteem/self-worth, and emotional reliance on others or a specific person (parent, partner, friend, child, etc.). People with codependency tend to lack boundaries and have a hard time setting boundaries with others. Increasing self-esteem and learning to set boundaries are two keys to overcoming codependency.

Resources

- Heather Brooke, LPC — heatherbrookelpc.com
- My Pain His Purpose Ministries — heatherbrookelpc.com/my-pain-his-purpose
- Trichotillomania Learning Center — bfrb.org
- *Where's My Hair? A Trichotillomania Story for Children* by Heather Meyer
- *Instead of Shame* by Debbie Wallace

HEATHER BROOKE is first and foremost a follower of Christ and mother to two amazing girls.

Heather accepted Christ as a middle school student, was Baptized in high school and rededicated her life to Christ privately in 2017 after recognizing spiritual warfare was part of narcissistic abuse she was experiencing and then again publicly in February 2024, after experiencing Christ moving in her life in a way she never had before.

Heather prides herself on trying to be a positive role model for her daughters, one who is a young adult and one who is a pre-teen. They love to travel and attend concerts together. Heather encouraged her oldest in competitive basketball until she decided she wanted to graduate high school a year early and pursue a career in some sort of ministry. Today, her oldest is currently attending cosmetology school and following the entrepreneurial footsteps of her mother, runs her own photography business. Heather's youngest is currently in middle school, finds her joy in competitive gymnastics and at the moment, hopes to compete at the collegiate level.

Throughout her professional career as a Licensed Professional Counselor and Neurofeedback Specialist, Heather has been recognized for her accomplishments in her field, including being inducted into Chi Sigma Iota National and Professional Honor Society, being inducted into the Marquis Who's Who in 2024, being invited to speak at professional conferences and seminars, and being nominated for VIP Jackson Magazine "Best in Jackson" in the Mental Health Professional category for 2024. In addition, Heather wrote her award-winning book, "Where's My Hair? A Trichotillomania Story for Children" in 2018. This book won her The InspireU Network's "Children's Author of 2023" award and was the first therapeutic book on the market for children. Heather is licensed as an LPC in Tennessee, Colorado and Georgia and is the owner of her own practice, Heather Brooke, LPC, LLC.

Heather is also the founder of My Pain His Purpose Ministries, a nonprofit whose mission is to share the love of Christ with others through personal testimonies and provide free and affordable mental health services to those in financial need. My Pain His Purpose holds seminars and conferences, in addition to having a podcast that allows people to share with others how God gave their pain purpose, the same way He gave Heather's pain purpose.

In addition to her professional career, Heather is a successful model, actress and beauty queen. She has been published in a number of magazines, walked runways in NY Fashion Week, LA, Denver, and Nashville, appeared on a billboard in Time Square, and is currently a brand ambassador for Hair Club, appearing in their infomercial and marketing. As an actor, Heather has appeared on national television shows such The Proposal and Masters of Illusion and had roles in independent short and feature films. Heather's pageant career has resulted in many awards including being crowned Ms. Woman Colorado United States 2017, being awarded Titleholder of the Year for Mrs. Colorado America 2011, Mrs. Colorado America's "Director's Choice" in 2013 and 2nd Runner-Up at Miss Tennessee for America Strong 2024. She is the reigning Miss West Tennessee for America 2025.

Keep Up with Heather

https://linktr.ee/HeatherBrookeLPC

Photo credits:
billymontanaimages.com
empire.edu/cosmetology-schools/colorado/aurora-denver

Follow our movement:

reigningresilientqueens.com

Fire Starting

Jenna Janisch

THE FIRST IMPACTFUL EVENT of being forged in the fire starts at my birth. The wound of abandonment was carved into my heart at three days old when I was given up for adoption by my biological mother. I was her second child, born into the world when she was only seventeen, and she had no biological father to rely on. As a neurodivergent teenager already struggling to care for herself and her year-old baby, she did the right thing by me by allowing someone else to raise me.

By the time I turned seventeen years old, I was able to understand this for the first time. But that didn't erase years of having the thought of not being good enough to be wanted by my own mother. That thought was planted into my head and took root. With my pale, freckled skin, I was adopted by a family where everyone else had brown hair, brown eyes, and darker skin. My hazel eyes and red hair stood out like the literal red-headed stepchild. I think even if my parents had never told me, I would have known early on I was different and didn't fit in with my family, just based on my looks. There is something deep down that happens to a child who never really fits in. This internal injury became a recurring theme for me at school, in social groups, and witnessing large families getting together; they all served as a constant reminder of how most of the world seemed to have deep bonds with home and family. I was different, an outcast: I had a unique life path, an assigned journey to finding that sense of home and belonging without the social and internal familial compass to guide me. Everywhere I looked, everywhere I went, I never felt a sense of belonging. I was good at sports, but not excellent. I was pretty but not skinny enough and different-looking with my red hair. I was smart but not nerdy enough. I had a few friends in every school clique but belonged to none. I was a loner in my home, in my school, in my heart. These instances just deepened the yearning within me too deeply to know myself and my roots, and to feel like I had found home.

From a young age, I was fascinated with religion, worship, the bible, and faith. I would beg to go to church and especially Sunday school, where I would hear stories of others who were outcasts and yet used for miracles, who felt lost and alone and were seen as worthy in the eyes of God. As I got older, I began experiencing New Age Christian worship, and my entire soul and body became activated. I remember feeling elevated and getting chills all over my body as I would stand and bathe in the magic of the music and the words that seemed to penetrate my mind with messages of hope. That hope trickled to that place in my heart center, lighting my mind and heart, and giving me the first sense of being filled with love. My mind was on fire to understand the man who came into the world and saw beauty in everyone. Finally, through these stories, I felt known and seen. I felt like someone else saw the world and the people the way I did. I felt deep hope and curiosity for each uniquely beautiful expression of God.

It was my church that took a group to Colorado on a ski trip to Breckenridge. This trip was truly significant to me in that I felt something I had never experienced before. I was alone on top of a snow-covered mountain with snow falling all around me and bright blue skies above me filled with big fluffy clouds. I was listening to my Walkman blast the Evanescence CD, and suddenly, alone on that mountain, I was overwhelmed with a sense of calm, of peace—a sensation I had gone more than sixteen years in the world without ever experiencing. A lightbulb clicked inside me, and it felt like a message to my soul that this was my home.

The mountains of Colorado held the peace and belonging I had been searching for my whole life. I returned to Arkansas after the trip and never gave up the hope and realization that if people lived in Colorado, one day I could too. It took me eleven more years to get there, but I am happy to say that as I write this, I am staring out the windows with a 360-degree view of snow-covered Rocky Mountains in a place I now get to aptly call home. But let's not get ahead of ourselves and skip the trail of tears, trauma, and heartbreak that led me there.

As I graduated high school, I was a year ahead of others my age. At seventeen, I went to college on a full-ride academic scholarship for nursing. I chose that focus originally because I wanted to please my adopted mother's desire for me to use my desire to help others with a "secure, high-demand job." That led me to two years of premedical studies, but eventually, my endless questioning and search to know myself outweighed my need for safety, and I changed my major to Psychology and Philosophy with a Liberal Arts minor. As I studied the great minds of the world and my long-unanswered questions, I identified myself as a tabula rasa, a blank slate endowed with the courage to decide who and what I wanted to be. As the first person in my biological and adopted family to go to college, I did not have a clear path to turn my desire to help others—my unwavering mind full of questions and yearning to know why and how about nearly everything—into a career. I graduated at twenty-one with a BS in Psychology, a minor in Philosophy, and with honors, College Scholar Cum Laude. Released into the world with a degree that basically gave me the skills to think too much and not be qualified to get paid well for anything, I explored jobs related to my interests.

My first job as a mental health aide and CNA at a state long-term facility allowed me to work with the severely mentally ill, the disabled, and those with end-of-life mental decline. My heart grew, and my services were honed as I rose in responsibility and became an activity leader for the Alzheimer's unit. I loved this role because I got to bring light and life to those who were often written off by their own family and friends because they were hard to have a continuous relationship with due to their lack of ability to retain new information.

I saw in them a sense of feeling alone, isolated, and unloved. I recognized this feeling and was able to bring love to those who had lost hope. I did everything I could, from spa days to shopping outings, game nights, physical activities, dance parties, and more to bring a sense of excitement to their now moments. I let them know they mattered deeply; if to no one else, they did to me. I wanted to show them that at that moment they were the most important thing in my world, and I was there to help them create a present moment worth living for.

As I gained experience and age, I found myself being drawn to make a change in my work and shift into working with the younger generation. I landed a job as a mental health paraprofessional working with kids who had behavior issues in the public school system.

I think part of me was ready to heal the inner child I felt was abandoned years ago; to see myself through the eyes of the teens and struggling children who had been labeled difficult and different. I worked with children from kindergarten to high school, and eventually landed full time in the "behavior classroom" filled with autistic children in elementary school. The time I spent in this position and learning to teach coping skills to these kids inspired me and grew my heart in ways that would prepare me for my future role as a mother in ways I never imagined. Just as things were settling, and I was feeling secure in my job and life, the first abusive relationship in my adult life came to shake things up.

On New Year's Eve, I met a man much older than me who was so charming and outgoing that I wanted to spend all my time with him. He had a large, close-knit family, which I had never experienced. He also had the familiar drinking problem I had been raised around. I assumed it to just be what all adults did; drink until drunk every day with friends. Within a few weeks, this man moved himself out of his sister's house into mine as I helped him rebuild his life, landing him a job and pouring my bleeding heart into his life. It fed my dreams to hopefully receive acceptance and love from him and his family.

I remember him saying so many awful things to me that I brushed under the rug, especially about my weight and how if I ever got heavier than I was then (a solid 135 pounds), he would leave me. Ladies, let me pause and tell you right now—if someone you are pouring into and rebuilding has the balls to say anything remotely like this to you, please take it as a huge red flag and run! Had I done so, I would have avoided the worst night of my life. This man lasted a good four months of using me for rides to work at the job I got for him, demeaning me, using me for housing and money, and slowly tearing me down and asserting his control over me and my life.

The whole relationship ended in a blowup one night as he came home drunk and found me on the phone with a male friend whom I had known for years. After getting off the phone with my friend, this man grabbed me by the throat, slammed me so hard into the wall it broke the sheetrock in the shape of my body, and he moved me into the closet, where he squeezed my neck so hard I began to lose consciousness. As I was fading out in what I was sure were my final moments of life, I remembered my phone was in my bra. Fumbling with it, I desperately called 911 for help.

We both got arrested for domestic violence that night, and my whole world got turned upside down. Enter job loss and major PTSD, and depression and anxiety at a level I had never known before. All things considered, I was alive but barely holding onto hope. How could someone do that to me?

Someone I thought I loved, someone I gave everything to? I was broken into a thousand pieces at twenty-two years old. As I struggled to leave my house for months following that encounter, I entered a dark depression. I began working for a law firm as a legal aid to assist me with getting the legal issues resolved from this incident. Over the next year, my name was cleared and the true story came to the surface, but not before a huge smear campaign and a deep dive into the darkness that comes after being a victim of domestic violence.

A couple of months later, I began getting messages from the younger brother of an acquaintance in high school who was heavily pursuing me. He was funny, his musical interests were similar to mine, and was deeply enamored by me. He had known about me and watched me as a cheerleader during our high school years, although I had never known him. Reluctantly, I decided to accept a date with him to encourage my heart to not harden indefinitely following the abuse I had endured. To let someone else show me that I was still worthy of being loved and appreciated.

This man became my first husband, but it was all wrong. Let me explain. I shared with him what had just happened. On our dates, I was honest about the deep fears I had around being a mother as he shared his desire to have a large family like the one he came from. Excited again about the possibility of being accepted into a big and strong family, I kept dating him when he would come to town on the weekends he was off work (which was on a job site several hours away). To me, this felt safe and would give me time to have my own space to settle back in while we got to know each other from a distance.

To my surprise, though, this man also had other plans for me. Over a holiday weekend, we took a group float trip down the river, and I drank too much while on the float and passed out on the ride home. I woke up in my bed not knowing how I got there and had been in an intimate situation I didn't agree to. Three weeks later, my world was turned upside down again. I was twenty-two and pregnant with someone I had known for two months.

Sometimes, the greatest challenges bring the most needed changes into your life. Before I go too much further into this story, I want to mention that in no way do I resent my son. I believe he has been an angel from the day he came into this world. He has shown me what real, unconditional love looks like. I would also like to say that the way and with whom I brought him into the world was not consensual and I was not prepared for the role of mother. But as an adopted girl, when I was given the news, I had no other choice. I was going to be a mother, after all.

We went to tell his family, and I was convinced by them to not have a "bastard" child and agreed I should marry their son. We got married when I was three months pregnant, and six months later, I brought my first child into the world. The birth was terrifying. I almost lost my son to birth complications, and I also almost lost my own life due to the traumatic surgical C-section that was required to save his blue and purple little body after laboring for 13.5 hours while the umbilical cord was wrapped *twice* around his neck.

The journey into motherhood was a relentless trial. I spun into postpartum depression without any mental health or community help, and felt the fear of being fat after birth becoming manifest. My body struggled to recover from such immense trauma. I was living in my worst fear. Money was scarce, I was in partnership with someone who imposed his will and desire for a family onto me, and I was not healed from anything that had happened. Now, this innocent child was dependent on me for literally everything in his life when I was struggling to just meet my own basic needs. I became a shell of a person.

Discovering that my husband was seeking outside sexual relationships broke me inside even more deeply. Within a year and a half of having my son, I filed for divorce, and again my reality crumbled around me. As my ex-husband moved out of my house and back into his parents' home, they worked together to kidnap my son, who was barely off the breast at the time. For over three months, I desperately petitioned the court, the police, and the prosecutor to help me see my son. Finally, an ex parte order was signed, giving me joint custody of my son, but not without significant scarring on my heart and emotional world yet again.

The months following my divorce filing were even worse than the night I almost died at the hands of my drunk ex-boyfriend. My ex-husband called all my friends and family and alienated me from everyone. He told me things like, "Our child would be better off if I was not in his life."

The extent of verbal and emotional abuse was so severe it sent me into a suicidal tailspin. Was he right? I could not imagine living a life without being a good mom to my baby. My heart was now outside my body, and I was being tormented with it.

Finally, in a moment of desperation, I reached out to a local therapist for help. This woman asked me the most influential question of my life in one of our first meetings. Besides properly diagnosing me with PTSD and validating my life experiences, she asked me, "Who are you Jenna? What do you like to do?"

As I struggled to answer with anything other than how I related to other people or to tell her about past activities I enjoyed as a child, I realized that, somehow, I had lost myself. Or maybe I had never known who I really was, and had spent my whole life trying to be what I thought others wanted me to be.

My life changed that day. I now had a purpose and direction to walk in. I was now on fire with curiosity to answer those questions and to fully know myself. That question ultimately led me to accept a job and move to Colorado to find peace again as I had on the ski mountain. But that's another chapter in another book. For this chapter, I leave you with that question for yourself. Who are you? How do you relate to others? What do you enjoy and dislike? How do you know? What is your I AM?

Fire Starting

Therapeutic Summary

In this chapter, Jenna experienced attachment issues as a result of her being given up by her birth mother and adopted, and experiencing domestic violence through physical, emotional, and sexual abuse and coercion, PTSD (including depression and anxiety) from her abuse and childbirth trauma, and postpartum depression following the birth of her child. As a result of the attachment issues that can often come from being adopted or just not developing a secure attachment in the first three years of life, Jenna was desperately seeking what she longed for in a family through her relationships with men, which ultimately led to toxic relationships. There is a possibility that Jenna could have been dealing with codependency as well. The PTSD from the assault and traumatic birth of her son is understandable, as is the depression and anxiety that came with the diagnosis. Postpartum depression is also common after experiencing a traumatic childbirth and complicated recovery. And as an accumulation of PTSD, postpartum depression, being cheated on, and going through a tumultuous divorce, suicidal ideation crept in.

Resources

- Suicide and Crisis Hotline — Dial/Text 988 988lifeline.org
- National Domestic Violence Hotline — 800-799-7233 thehotline.org
- Postpartum Support International — postpartum.net
- Counseling/Therapy — psychologytoday.com

JENNA identifies as she/her/them. As a child, she was adopted, and as an adult, she studied Psychology and Philosophy and went on to study education in graduate school. Jenna always knew she wanted to be a helper and a healer and knew she was definitely a different breed in the world. She sought to understand and teach, not only herself, but other seekers, too. The way she stood out among the crowd, and was different as a channel, was apparent very early on in childhood and has been the resounding theme throughout all of her life.

Jenna moved to Denver, Colorado, from Arkansas over nine years ago. She was attuned as a Reiki Master in Denver in 2016 and attained her 200 RYT in 2019. In 2021, she achieved advanced practitioner status for reading the Akashic Records from Linda Howe.

From her training, her connection as a channel and guide continued to grow. From participating in metaphysical fairs to throwing spiritual events, one of her companies, Into the Ether, began to take form. She eventually decided to curate a space for a beautiful mountain community in Colorado after more than thirteen years of spiritual study. Jenna is ready to help you connect with the Big Energy and use her story to help others know that all roads lead to home when you follow your heart.

Keep Up with Jenna

https://linktr.ee/Intotheether

Photo credits:
d20photography.com
empire.edu/cosmetology-schools/colorado/aurora-denver

Follow our movement:

reigningresilientqueens.com

Halfway Dead

Kalena Rodriguez

DEATH IS THE SPIRIT, *or soul, leaving the body; without the spirit the body is dead.* Physically, we are expecting death when our heart stops and we never take another breath as our family and loved ones mourn their loss. We are what is believed to be freed, living our best afterlife.

My defense attorney, a white man with red hair in a wrinkled suit, approached me in the courtroom with news of a plea deal the district attorney was willing to offer me; ninety-six years for a violent crime I was accused of committing. My body froze, my heart stopped, and I'm almost positive that if I had a soul back then, it was completely gone.

I felt like I was a lost soul since I had been sexually assaulted from the time I was eight through fourteen by my grandmother's boyfriend. With the many years of abuse at a young age, I still felt I had a fight left in me to live;

however, learning of a ninety-six-year sentence was the closest thing to dying I had felt up to that point. I had no fight left in me; all hope was gone. I walked around for three days alone, cold and mourning the loss of me, still trying to make my way through the world of gangs and drugs that I was woven into.

I felt the heat of the barrel from a 45-caliber gun against my head. All thoughts were gone other than *This is it*. I was already dead. I would finally be set free, taking all my pain away that had lived free in my mind for a decade. Everything was so noisy. My boyfriend was screaming at me, "Tell me where she is, Kalena, or we are going to kill you! You are supposed to be loyal to me."

The "she" he was referring to was a good friend of mine. My boyfriend's business partner had shot her baby's dad a week before this night, and the victim survived the shot. My boyfriend was ordered to find him through me because people found out I knew his kid's mom.

The crime I was accused of was beating a woman over owing me money. I vowed to never hurt another female again (I never have). I already felt dead. I was not going to allow a man to convince me to directly or indirectly hurt someone again. I would rather die.

BOOM

The trigger was pulled, and all the noise went away. Despite my eardrums being blown out, I heard someone say, "It's not over yet. Keep fighting."

The 45 had backfired from being used too much prior to this shot. Instead of the man I trusted with my life letting up, he continued to beat me with the cold steel. I could feel the blood dripping down my face. I do not have any explanation for how I survived being brutally beaten by my gang enforcer boyfriend other than I was covered in the blood of Christ.

The night my body should have died, my evil mind died instead, and I was born again. I woke up in the hospital a few days after my attack, to the most handsome boy I've ever seen. And I knew I loved him because I had an overwhelming feeling of happiness and pure joy. I did not know he was my three-and-half-year-old son Anthony. I could not remember anything about him. Along with my many bruises, swollen face, and broken ribs, I had developed retrograde amnesia due to brain trauma. I remember nothing, not even the crime I was said to have committed (which I did do).

The next three years on bond were a struggle for me. I feared everything. Some nights, I would hide behind my door with a 12-gauge just in case someone was coming back to finish the job. I could hear my mom crying and praying to God to help me. She didn't know what to do. My mom always believed I was going to do great things, even in the darkest times. The special guest at church, Bishop T. D. Jakes, a large, bold, African American man whose voice was as soft as an angel's and could be as fierce and mighty as a lion, laid his healing hands on me when I was fifteen. He didn't know I had been withdrawing from drugs, trying to fight my demons. He powerfully announced, "When you are walking in your purpose, you are going to do great things."

If my mom had any doubts about me, T. D. Jakes confirmed for her God's light was going to shine through me.

After the beating, I understood nothing. People were trying to tell me stories so I could remember things about my life and who I was. To be quite honest, I hated the person people were describing. I did not know who I was, and my life seemed to have no meaning.

During my sexual abuse, to help me cope with what was going on, I developed a terrible drinking habit that quickly turned me into an alcoholic at a young age. My mom would take me to a church after a long night of drinking to wash me clean, thinking that I needed Jesus. To me, then, Jesus was just another man with high expectations and low performance.

As I was healing from my brain trauma, I decided to go to a familiar place. For some reason, I remembered the church my mom would take me to. I immediately felt peace in my heart, and I could breathe again. Prior to this, I felt my body had stopped. They say that your mind continues to work for seven minutes after your heart stops and your body dies. I like to believe my body was tired from all I was putting it through. My mind needed to be wiped clean from all the trauma I had to go through at a young age. My heart was broken from it. God gave me the chance to start over. I began to live the new life I was given.

Meanwhile, on bond, I had two more baby boys. Gauge was born in 2012. His name came from the gun I gave up that was tangibly keeping me safe. Then came Justus in 2013. His name has a lot of meanings behind it. I had a mentality of not snitching, so I never told on the people who hurt me. But I still wanted them to have consequences. God gave me my Justus.

The day came when I finally had to face the consequences for my actions. On February 25, 2014, my trial started for ten state charges: second-degree kidnapping, two second-degree assault charges, torture, robbery, false imprisonment, and five conspiracies. If I lost the trial, I would be spending 240 years in prison. Life! I was confident I was not going to get sentenced to this much time. I knew there was no way that God would keep me safe just to end it. During a cross-examination with my female codefendant, the DA brought in information that was not proven factual about me selling drugs to the victim. My attorney moved for a mistrial. Although my attorney knew it was not going to stand, it scared the DA enough. Thinking that I was going to walk away scot-free, they offered me a deal of ten to twelve years in prison. My mind still couldn't wrap itself around being guilty because I honestly could not remember being guilty. Deep down, I knew I was, so I took the deal after much convincing by my attorneys that it was the best thing possible. The right-hand man said to me, "Kalena, I want to have a conversation within ten years in person in my office fighting for other people's lives, not you calling me from prison fighting for yours." I took the deal and went home to say goodbye to my babies. My son Anthony (four years old) cried in a way I have never heard anyone cry, and it still haunts me. I told him I would be home before he was ten, a promise I didn't know if I could keep.

I was taken into custody on February 27, 2014. On June 6, 2014, I was sentenced. The judge said, "Kalena, I watched you walk in my courtroom without a heart, one of the coldest, cutthroat people I've encountered in my entire career. I watched you go through a traumatic event, two pregnancies, and I watched you grow into a beautiful, kindhearted woman who is going to do great things. Unfortunately, our actions have consequences. I am now sentencing you to the Colorado Department of Corrections for eleven years. But you are not a lost soul. It's not over yet. Keep fighting."

I knew at that point God had been with me from the beginning.

Going to prison and being away from my kids was the hardest thing I have ever done. A lot of things in my life were negative. I knew I was a good mom and loved my boys with all my heart and would make sure they knew that I did, no matter where I was. Thankfully, I had an incredible support system, and my mom helped keep my children together. I had to be grateful for the prison time I got (and the time I didn't get) and focus on getting through the fire and obstacles that were in front of me. I learned that I was not who I used to be. I created a solid foundation of God, fitness, and family that became my structure. Helping others and community became the way I would move into my purpose. I moved through my day the way I wanted to live outside, and lived that way inside.

I served more than four years of my eleven-year sentence in prison, and was released to a halfway house on May 25, 2018, for seven months. I was paroled on December 18, 2018. My goal was to always go back to the prison I was released from and help the women behind the walls grow with hope and help them with their freedom. I like to call it Lifting the Yard.

I created a nonprofit called K. Project Freedom. We help incarcerated individuals become free from the inside out. At K. Project Freedom, our mission extends beyond breaking the chains of recidivism. We are dedicated to addressing a spectrum of challenges faced by our participants, including addiction recovery, mental health support, secure housing, gainful employment, access to clothing and nourishment, educational courses and certifications, as well as engaging in sober activities and promoting prosocial behavior. With an unwavering commitment to dismantling the cycles of recidivism, addiction, and mental health struggles prevalent in Colorado, K. Project Freedom stands as a beacon of hope, actively working toward a brighter, more rehabilitative future for our community members in need.

I had another baby boy, Patricio "Junior." He completed my world and family. I have an extra son, too. God blessed our family with JoJo, Anthony's best friend. His family had some struggles, and we were in a place to support JoJo's needs. Yup, that's right, *all* boys. An Asian woman told me when I was pregnant with Junior that in her culture, they believe having four boys is lucky. When she told me that, I took a Nicki Minaj line, "No, I'm not lucky, I'm blessed." I now say I have five boys with the addition of JoJo. Years later, an Asian man told me that in his culture, they believe four boys are lucky and five boys are a gang. I responded, "My belief is five boys is an army of God."

When I walked out of prison, I started working with an attorney as a paralegal. We encountered many different walks of life. We met with a client one night at a restaurant. That client looked at me with such amazement and uplifted my soul with all her compliments. She introduced me to the modeling world, and I flourished like never before. I had the opportunity to walk on a runway in New York for New York Fashion Week. Not wanting to get blinded by the fame and glory of the world, I still had to move with the purpose God had for me to help people. It was suggested that I try to be Ms. Colorado.

Most people's description of me might include the word beautiful. I *am* confident, do not get me wrong, though at times, I can be insecure. In my head, I was saying, *How? I'm a felon. What if they say no? What if I'm not pretty enough or skinny enough, and what if I fail?* Then I stood up tall, remembering I am a child of God, and said, *So what if I do fail? I'll do it again! So what if I am a felon. I have made mistakes! I am beautiful inside and out. If they tell me no that's not okay; it won't be the first time and it won't be the last. But at least I tried, so that's a win.*

After all that self-talk, I decided I was going to try to be International United Miss Colorado. Despite my felony, despite my pain, despite my insecurities, despite all the odds against me, I became the reigning 2021/2022 International United Ms. Colorado, working with prisons and being a voice for those behind the walls. However, despite all my accomplishments and my family being whole, I felt something was missing from my heart. I still had a void that wasn't yet filled; the pain from the night my mind died and my spirit was recreated.

Where were the men who hurt me? Still, they took up space in my mind. I realized I needed to forgive them, and God knew I was ready. I opened my direct messages on my phone, and I had a message from the man who hurt me. My heart sank into my stomach, and I thought I was going to pass out from disbelief. All I could do was smile and look up and say, "Ok, God, I hear you." I quickly responded. I learned he had been on dialysis for five years. His kidneys were failing. My first thought was that karma *is a bitch*, then I realized that was not the reason for the interaction, and I needed to humble myself because he was still a human. I agreed to meet up with him. My mom was scared to death, but I wasn't afraid anymore. It was for something bigger than me, and I needed to do it. I wanted to fully heal. I found out fast what his reason for meeting me was. It was to save his life and give him my kidney. Some thought I was nuts. Why the hell would I save a man who nearly killed me? My answer was simple. Although he almost killed my flesh, he actually saved me. If he hadn't done what he did, I wouldn't have had the opportunity to grow into who I am today and have the ability to live free.

At that moment I knew I had truly forgiven him, and I was finally able to take back full control of my life. God is funny though. I went through the process to donate my kidney to him. I hadn't heard from him for about a week, and I thought he might have gone to jail. I got a call from him. He had been rushed to the hospital. The doctors had matched him before my paperwork was processed, and he already had a kidney donor. "It's the thought that counts" means something different to me now. My intentions are pure, my heart is filled. I continue to grow my legacy of not allowing the pain I have caused in my life or felt to be in vain.

"To all who mourn in Israel he will give a crown of beauty for ashes, a joyous blessing instead of mourning, festive praise instead of despair. In their righteousness they will be like great oaks that the Lord has planted for his own glory." —Isaiah 61:3 – New Living Translation (NLT)

Beauty from ashes represents God's redemptive power from the very beginning. When people thought they could bury me, they didn't know I was a seed of Jesus, and I would rise! With death comes new life. "It's not over. Keep fighting."

Therapeutic Summary

In this chapter, Kalena documents surviving a number of traumatic events that led to post-traumatic stress disorder (PTSD): sexual abuse, the violence of being in a gang, being beaten, and physical brain trauma. In addition to the trauma, Kalena experienced substance abuse issues, anxiety, and possible depression, as well as low self-worth. Trauma and PTSD itself can lead to anxiety, depression, substance abuse, and self-esteem issues. But in addition to the trauma, Kalena was facing situational anxiety and depression while waiting on sentencing and spending time in prison being away from her family.

Resources

- Neurofeedback — eeginfo.com, heatherbrookelpc.com
- Built to Recover — builttorecover.com
- K. Project Freedom — kprojectfreedom.com

I GREW UP POOR in a one-parent household, and there were a lot of struggles and obstacles we had to face. With my sister's mental health issues, the responsibility of my niece became my own at fourteen. I had never worked before, so I quickly turned to the streets to sell drugs for a quick income. I learned at a young age how to make money and care for my family. Despite my good intentions, it would lead me to near death and incarceration. Although I was raised with good morals and values that were directed negatively for a long time, finally finding my way through trauma, pain, and God, I was able to rise above and use His love to mend my mind, body, and soul. I was able to turn pain into a platform to persevere. I have achieved a lot over the years that I am proud of, the most important being that I am a mother of four handsome boys. I have not always been the best mother, but my sons know they are loved, and I would stand by them through anything like my Father (God) did for me. "True love never fails."

Keep Up with Kalena

https://linktr.ee/kalenarod

Photo credits:
d20photography.com
empire.edu/cosmetology-schools/colorado/aurora-denver

Follow our movement:

reigningresilientqueens.com

I Have Good News, and I Have Bad News

Karleen Wagner

AT THIRTY-EIGHT YEARS OLD, I enjoyed life as a wife and mom. We were your average family living in the suburbs. My husband, our two boys, and I were all training in martial arts at the time. When my kids attended school full time, I found a new career as a martial artist. Not only did I train, but I also taught classes and ran the academy we trained at. I also ran my own program through our local recreation center and empowered many children through their training. I was in my element and enjoying every minute of it. I was in the best shape I had ever been, and honestly, I felt pretty good! Until I didn't ... I slowly began noticing that it took longer for me to recover after training. I was also tired during the day, yet I couldn't sleep well at night. It was harder for me to take a deep breath when I exerted myself, and I was experiencing some back pain. I look back now and realize that I probably was also suffering from depression. I didn't want to socialize; just getting to work became a challenge when it used to be such a joy. My friends and neighbors began to wonder where I had disappeared to.

I finally went to see my primary care doctor. Just to make a long story short, he was no help. Over the course of two years, the only test he did was a finger-prick iron test. I have always been anemic, so receiving that result was not a surprise. For two years, I heard him tell me, "As we get older, things just don't work the way they used to." At thirty-eight, I didn't see myself as old.

I had begun researching my symptoms, and it appeared I might have thyroid problems. So, I made an appointment with my gynecologist for an annual exam. I told him how I was feeling and what I thought it might be. He agreed that it could be thyroid related, and ordered a full blood workup to include blood count, hormones, liver and kidney function, and more. From the outside, I appeared to be perfectly healthy, but we were both in for a shock.

Have you ever received "the call"? The one where you received news that would forever change the trajectory of your life? This was one of those calls. It was my doctor on the other line, and he said, "I have good news, and I have bad news."

"Well, okay, give me the good news."

The good news was that my thyroid was fine. The bad news . . . My kidneys were at 22 percent of their full function. *What? How could that be? I've never had kidney problems!*

I was shocked to hear that news. While it was nothing I had ever expected to hear, at 22 percent, we had to quickly find answers. I didn't have time to sit and think about what kidney failure meant; we needed to figure out why an otherwise healthy forty-year-old was in kidney failure.

I was referred to another primary care doctor, and she immediately ordered multiple blood tests, MRIs, ultrasounds, and a twenty-four-hour urine collection. After we got the results from all the tests back, I finally had a diagnosis: polycystic kidney disease (PKD). I still think it is unbelievable that my primary doctor missed the diagnosis of kidney failure! This is when I learned that you have to be your own advocate when it comes to your health and the health of your loved ones.

Some things I learned about PKD:

1. It's genetic (except when it's not, more about that later).
2. There is no slowing it down (however, now some promising treatments are available).
3. There is no cure.
4. The treatments to extend your life include dialysis and kidney transplant.
5. Left untreated, it will lead to full kidney failure and death.

Well, at least I now had a name to go with this disease that was shutting down my kidneys. The first thing I found interesting was the fact that no one in my family has this disease. Since I had no family history, I was a mutation. However, being a mutation did not spare me from passing it on to one or both of my boys. As of this writing, neither have been formally tested, but we believe at least one of them has it. This was more heartbreaking to me than when I found out I was in kidney failure because of it. It bears the question, *If I had known ... would we have had kids?* I don't have an answer for that. I believe God blessed us with both of our boys, and He already knew what the outcome would be.

A quick anatomy and genetic lesson about PKD and the kidneys. When you have PKD, your kidneys develop cysts from within the kidney tissue. These are not cancerous, and they are not formed from something on the outside attacking them. Eventually, these cysts overwhelm the nephrons (the structures in the kidneys that filter the blood and produce urine), and your kidneys begin to fail. Kidneys with PKD are enlarged due to the size of the cysts. Typical kidneys are the size of a fist. Polycystic kidneys can be as large as a football and weigh up to thirty pounds each. Often, those with advanced

PKD may look pregnant. Mine are each about the size of a Nerf football, and they both still reside in my body. A common misconception is that the native kidneys are removed when you receive a transplant, however that usually is not the case. The exceptions being if they are cancerous, necrotic, or causing other medical difficulties. The surgery to remove kidneys as large as mine comes with more risk than leaving them in. Transplanted kidneys are placed in the front of your abdomen, in the groin area. I love playing two truths and a lie with people I don't know; I always say I have 3 kidneys. Which is not a lie! Should I need another transplant, I would have a fourth kidney placed on the other side of my abdomen.

Even after finding the cause of my kidney failure, I didn't have time to dwell on it. At 22 percent and dropping, I was already eligible to go on the kidney transplant list. Right away, I had more testing performed to see if I was healthy enough for a transplant, and we began talking about dialysis. Oddly enough, my sister-in-law had been through two kidney transplants. The first one failed miserably, and the second one was truly lifesaving. My husband remembers the years of dialysis she went through and how hard it was on her and the family. I was a little scared of dialysis and how it would not only affect my body, but also affect my family. I was most concerned about my boys, who were nine and eleven when I was diagnosed. At the time, the wait list for a kidney was three to five years. I was seeing all of the "ologists"; nephrologists, psychologists, cardiologists, neurologists, and some I've probably forgotten. At one point, one of the transplant nurses suggested to me that I look for a living donor. I was young and otherwise healthy, and it would be better if I didn't have to go on dialysis.

Well, this was a whole new adventure. Before this experience, I was definitely the person who was better at giving than receiving. I didn't ask for help often but was always willing to lend a hand to others. God was about to teach me a huge lesson about learning to receive. For me to find a living donor, I would have to ask for one. Sounds simple enough … or not. I would literally be asking someone to go under the knife for me and give me a piece of themselves. That is a BIG ask!

What finally helped me swallow my pride and humble myself was knowing that asking for a living donor was going to give me the best outcome for my health. I wanted to not only be around for my boys, I wanted to be healthy enough that I could live life with them, and not just sit on the sidelines. I wanted everything life could offer, and I didn't want to be hindered by dialysis. So, I asked. I asked at the martial arts academy; I asked at church; I asked my friends; I even posted it on Facebook. I was deeply humbled when I had ten people offer to get tested to see if they would be a match. There really are no words for how I felt. A couple of the people who offered, I didn't even know. They were friends of a friend.

I heard stories about why these people wanted to donate to me. Their stories could fill another chapter. I was blessed beyond measure. Now it was time for everyone to start the application process and begin the testing to find a match. The first person to fill out an application and get tested ended up being a match. This is almost unheard of; I knew I was once again seeing the hand of God at work. My match was a young lady I had spent the previous few years mentoring and becoming friends with. I met her at the martial arts academy I trained and worked at. She is nineteen years younger than me, and I was concerned about how donating a kidney would affect her future. Would she be able to have kids? Were there any long-term results of her having only one kidney for the majority of her life? The transplant team assured me that she would be fine and that I should accept the kidney.

During this time period, I found that I was relatively calm. I was the one telling everyone else not to worry, that everything was going to be okay. I am definitely a doer, and since everything happened so fast, I was in go-mode. I got done what had to get done. There wasn't a lot of downtime to think about it. I have told my husband and kids often that if they could have been inside my mind, they would have seen how calm I was. I truly believe that God gave me this peace and was with me through every step of the process.

In under a year from the time I was diagnosed, we were in the hospital for the transplant surgery. I was at 8 percent function at the time of the transplant, and had managed to stay off of dialysis. My parents came into town to help with the boys while I was in the hospital and recovering at home. The day of the surgery, I had friends and family at the hospital with me as my donor and I were being prepped. I could not have gone through all of this without the support of my family and friends. Community has always been very important to me; little did I know how much I would rely on that community to be by my side during all of this.

The transplant was a success! After four days in the hospital, my donor and I were released to go home. Our time in the hospital was short, but we had many visitors. My friends and family were so grateful for her gift to me, and her friends and family were so supportive of her bravery and generosity. We were both showered with love and support. Having received a healthy and working kidney, I started feeling better within a few days. I was still healing from surgery but felt more energetic and was sleeping better already. My donor's body was now adjusting to having only one kidney and also healing from surgery. This type of surgery is actually harder on the donor than on the recipient, which is another reason I had a hard time asking someone to go through this for me. In the end, she recovered fully and is continuing to live a full and thriving life!

I can never repay her for her gift. I feel like words always fall short of the magnitude of my gratitude for her. She not only gave me the gift of life, but she also gave my boys a healthy mom, and my husband a wife to grow old with. I love this quote by John Bunyan, "You have never really lived until you have done something for someone who can never repay you." This is what my donor has done for me. She has truly lived.

As of the writing of this chapter, I am celebrating twelve years post-transplant. My friend's kidney has found a home in my body, and I am choosing to live a thriving life. As a Christian, I believe that in all situations, God is in control. I have had many things happen in my life that were unwanted and unexpected. Some were because of choices I'd made; some were the result of the choices of others, and some just happened without warning or explanation. The news of kidney failure fell into the last category. This definitely was *not* part of my life plan.

Some things I learned from this experience:

1. Life Happens! If you go through life thinking that the unwanted and unexpected won't happen to you, you will be very disappointed (and possibly angry) when it does. We can't expect life to go by without incident, no matter how much we try to maintain control. We are able to control many things with our lifestyle and the choices we make, but there are also things that just happen.

    In the book, *The 7 Laws of Enough: Cultivating a Life of Sustainable Abundance*, authors Gina LaRoche and Jennifer Cohen tell us that when the unexpected happens, rather than asking "why me," we should come from the perspective of "why not me?" When we think "why me," we are automatically putting ourselves into the mindset of being a victim. When we think "why not me," we position ourselves to be a victor instead! I want to remind you of another truth: Even though we are not exempt from bad things happening, we are also not exempt from the good. Don't be *so* stuck in the bad that you are missing out on the good that the world has for you.

2. Be your own advocate in health and in life. I now take classes and do a lot of research about how to create better health in my own life so that I can keep this kidney strong for as long as possible. Through my own experience, and all that I have learned, I have now found a new career as a health and wellness strategist. I help others to create daily healthy habits to support physical, mental, emotional, and spiritual health.

3. Giving and receiving are reciprocal. Without one, the other cannot exist. In order for someone to give, there needs to be someone willing to receive, and it works the opposite way as well. I realized it gave me great joy to give, but if someone did not want to receive, that joy

was diminished. I also knew that I would be taking away someone else's joy if I refused to receive as I had done so many times. It is okay to need help, to ask for help, and to receive help. I still have a huge heart to give, but I now understand the importance of also receiving.

4. When life gives you lemons, make lemonade! We've all heard this phrase. I find it to be very empowering. I knew my life was going to change. For the rest of my life, I will be on medications to suppress my immune system so that my gifted kidney will survive. These medications are necessary, but there are side effects. Being immunosuppressed means that I have a higher risk of illness than the average person. I have to watch the foods I eat, the surroundings I'm in, and I need to pay attention to the smallest evidence of any illness. If I wait too long to receive care when I am sick, it could damage my transplant.

However, this experience has led me on a new path, a new career, and opened up new opportunities. I am an author and speaker. I own three businesses and have the pleasure of encouraging and supporting others in their dreams. I have the opportunity to share my journey so that others may learn from it, be encouraged by it, and be able to move forward in their own lives as a result. I'm not sure I would be where I am had I not gone through this experience.

My life has changed, and that change has been good. Had I tried to reclaim all that I had lost, I would be living stuck in the past. It is hard to see what opportunities lie ahead when you are constantly looking behind. Life sucks sometimes. Sometimes, we need to take time to grieve. Sometimes, we need to take time to heal. My encouragement to you is not to take up a long residency in those places. Take the time you need, but then turn your eyes to the future. Life is full of choices. You have the choice to merely survive or to thrive! I hope you join me in a thriving life!

Therapeutic Summary

In this chapter, Karleen mentions the possibility of depression, even though it wasn't diagnosed. She mentions feeling exhausted during the day, difficulty sleeping at night, losing interest in the things she enjoyed and not being as social, in addition to lacking joy; all of which can be symptoms of depression. As a result of her Polycystic Kidney Disease (PKD) diagnosis, Karleen's depression could have worsened. She might have also experienced anxiety during this time. Karleen reports she leaned on her faith and trust in God, and in place of potential depression and anxiety, she experienced peace and calmness that moved her through the healing process. Karleen's experience most likely won't be everyone's experience with a serious health issue and diagnosis. It is completely normal to experience a level of grief, anger, depression, and anxiety with a diagnosis of this caliber. If you have found yourself feeling that way, know that is normal and it is okay. Give yourself grace as you process and work through your healing journey.

Resources

- Counseling/Therapy — psychologytoday.com
- National Kidney Foundation — kidney.org
- The PKD Foundation — pkdcure.org
- Register to be an Organ Donor — donatelife.net
- Organ Transplant Information — unos.org/transplant

Karleen is a Colorado Native and has been happily married since 1995. She and her husband have two adult children and are currently enjoying life as empty nesters!

In 2011, a personal health crisis served as a wake-up call for her, prompting a significant lifestyle reevaluation. Her journey toward improved physical, mental, and emotional well-being has given life to a new passion to help others move past merely surviving into a life where they thrive!

Her company, Choosing to Thrive, embodies the belief that we have a choice in how we show up in this world; we can choose to thrive or just survive.

Karleen is an entrepreneur, speaker, author, and podcast guest.

Keep Up with Karleen

https://linktr.ee/choosing_to_thrive

Photo credits:
d20photography.com
empire.edu/cosmetology-schools/colorado/aurora-denver

Follow our movement:

reigningresilientqueens.com

The Power within the Ordinary

Laura Farley

I AM HERE AS A BEACON of everyday resilience and unassuming charm. This story weaves a narrative that speaks not of grand gestures or dramatic events but of the beautifully mundane moments that shape our lives. My tale is one of quiet triumphs and gentle victories, where the subtle nuances of human connection and the simple joys of existence take center stage. I hope through my lens, you can find yourself reflecting on the ordinary yet profound experiences that make up the tapestry of our shared humanity and know that every story matters. In the words of J. R. R. Tolkien, "It is no bad thing to celebrate a simple life" because extraordinary things can come of it.

As I stand in Coloradough Pizza, surrounded by the familiar sights and sounds of my thriving business, I can't help but reflect on the journey that has brought me here. Starting this company from scratch, with no safety net to catch me if I fell, has been the most daunting yet exhilarating experience of my life. I am remembering the sleepless nights, the endless doubts, and the relentless determination that fueled me to push forward against all odds.

I recall the early days when I had nothing but a vision and a deep conviction in my idea. It was a leap of faith, a risky venture that required me to invest my time, energy, and resources without the guarantee of success. I faced countless challenges, made numerous mistakes, and weathered setbacks that tested my resilience at every turn. But through it all, I persevered, learning and growing with each obstacle I overcame.

Upon these reflections, I can't help but let my mind wander back to the girl who was teased, manipulated, and bullied in high school, and to her strength for always pushing through to one more day. Experiencing high school with all of its highs and lows can be daunting for any teenager. I had an amazing core group of friends and activities to keep me happy and busy, but there were still days of lunches eaten hidden in the bathroom and the awkward waiting till everyone was out of the locker rooms in order to change for gym class, so no one could make fun of my body.

Almost every young girl struggles with body image. That can carry on into adulthood, causing mental, social, and physical ailments. I got teased mercilessly about how tall I was because I was 5'8" in 7th and 8th grade. My dental adventures with braces, surgeries, implants, and ridiculous metal bars in my mouth (that would sometimes get stuck and prop my mouth open) were endless sources of material for boys and girls to hurl at me. Wearing baggy clothes and sitting with pillows covering my midsection was how I would feel comfortable and secure because of how my body was made fun of and how I started to perceive all of its flaws. My bullies' names and faces were etched into my mind for the longest time, and their words would still ring in my ears in certain situations. I was never driven to self-harm, but those thoughts were never far from my mind.

It seems that pivotal points in our lives are always such clear and vivid memories. One of my high school harassers will never know the truly profound and positive effect that they had on my life.

Fast-forward to college, as I was enjoying a beautiful day on Denver's Metropolitan State University campus, when I looked up and my blood ran cold. One of my main tormentors from high school was walking straight for me. Our eyes met, and a small cruel curl of their lip made it clear that their intentions were not good. I was immediately aware again of superficial imperfections of my body and the fact that I was alone. Tears welled in my eyes as anxiety set in. I shook. In a panic, the scared and traumatized girl inside of me scrambled for a lifeline and turned to the closest person at a neighboring table and begged them to engage in a conversation. That poor, startled guy would later become the one I ran a pizza empire with.

He was sitting with a book in his hand and a confused look on his face due to my odd request. He shrugged his shoulders at me. I just started rambling on about any topic that came into my head; the day, classes, I even asked him if he couldn't see well since he was wearing glasses. This man's tolerance and patience during my ramblings would bleed over to our professional partnership one day. When the coast was clear, we both packed up our school supplies and headed off to class—the same class. We would later find out that we had four classes together that semester. Our friendship was forged quickly.

As we were both criminal justice majors with dreams of working for law enforcement, neither one of us thought that owning and operating a successful pizza business together would be in our future. After a time when I was working in retail and he was working in law enforcement, we came to the decision that we wanted to work for ourselves and start something that we could be proud of. Coloradough Pizza began.

When we started the business, it was tumultuous. It was interesting to learn all the things we didn't know. One of the hardest parts of starting the business was letting go of fears and doubts caused by experiences or learned behavior from my past. I clung to memories of failure like a lifeline, afraid to release them for fear of losing a part of myself. But I soon realized that holding onto what had been no longer served me. It only weighed me down, and the doubt was preventing me from moving forward. This felt true from both the personal and professional standpoint. So, I made a conscious decision to release the past, to thank it for the lessons it taught me, and to set my sights on the future. I decided to buckle down, and I made the following list to guide me in the professional and personal growth that was surrounding the start of Coloradough Pizza, and to hold me accountable for my actions or lack thereof.

First and foremost, remember the importance of vision and clarity. Define what you want to achieve or overcome and create a vision for where you see yourself heading. This will give you direction and motivation to keep moving forward, even when faced with obstacles.

Next, embrace the power of resilience. Reflect on the times in your business when things didn't go as planned and how you bounced back from setbacks. It is so easy to get derailed if something doesn't go our way. We need to remember that setbacks are a part of life, and it's how you respond to them that shapes your journey. Stay determined, keep a positive mindset, and believe in your ability to overcome challenges.

Adaptability is another key lesson to bring into your business journey. In the business world, you have to adapt to changing circumstances, market trends, and competition to stay ahead. Applying this flexibility allows you to be open to new approaches, willing to try different strategies, and ready to pivot when needed. Embracing change and being adaptable will help you navigate through difficult times more effectively.

Don't forget the importance of self-care and balance. In the midst of running a business, it's easy to neglect your well-being and personal needs. Remember to prioritize self-care during your personal struggles. Take time for yourself, practice self-compassion, and seek support from loved ones or professionals if needed. Taking care of yourself physically, emotionally, and mentally will give you the strength to face challenges head on.

Lastly, trust in your own abilities and believe in your resilience. Negative self-talk and making excuses for why things fail or never get started is an easy pit to fall into. You need to trust that you have the skills, knowledge, and inner strength to navigate through difficult times and come out stronger on the other side.

By applying these lessons learned in your business journey, you can approach challenges with a sense of empowerment, purpose, and determination. Remember that you can build your business from the ground up, because you have had the capacity to rebuild and renew your life after hardship, drawing on the skills and resilience you've cultivated along the way. To all the women out there who are considering starting a business, I offer this advice: believe in yourself and your abilities. You are capable of achieving anything you set your mind to, and the world is waiting for you to unleash your potential. Don't let fear or self-doubt hold you back. Instead, let them fuel your determination and drive.

Over the years, Coloradough Pizza has quickly captured the hearts and taste buds of the local community, and it has been transformed into a beloved neighborhood staple. It was easy to use the shop as a platform for philanthropy through pizza, and this business became the ground floor for my heavy involvement in volunteering and giving back to the community that supports us. Hosting fundraisers and spearheading donation drives for local schools and charities makes my heart happy and full and gives me a purpose other than running a business.

As I navigated this path of opening a business as well as self-discovery, I realized that I wasn't alone. There were countless women out there going through the same struggles, battling the same demons, and trying to accomplish the same things. And in that realization of knowing I wasn't alone, I realized that neither were they. In our darkest moments, we feel as if the weight of the world rests solely on our shoulders and we think no one else can relate. We are wrong. We stand together. Our emotions are not a sign of weakness but a testament to our strength and resilience.

Looking back on the journey I have taken, I realized something that I think is very important not only for myself but for other people as well. A lot of us compare our life experience to other people's, and sometimes we feel that if our stories don't involve trauma or something terrible happening to us, that our stories don't matter or they are not as important to anyone else. I will tell you that we are still powerful, that we still learn and teach, and that our stories and voices matter. You are the unsung hero, the quiet force that moves mountains with your mere presence. In a world that glorifies grand achievements and extraordinary feats, your one-step-at-a-time achievements are an example for those who find magic in the simple act of being themselves.

In a world that often glorifies exceptionalism, it's easy to overlook the hidden power of mediocrity. But within the realm of ordinary lies a strength that is often underestimated and underappreciated. It's in the everyday moments, the mundane tasks, and the unspectacular achievements that true resilience and endurance can be found.

Embracing mediocrity does not mean settling for less or giving up on striving for greatness. Instead, it's about recognizing the value in the small victories, the incremental progress, and the consistent effort that often goes unnoticed. It's about finding strength in consistency, perseverance, and reliability.

In this very mediocrity, character is built, relationships are nurtured, and success is sustained over the long haul. It is the steady pace of mediocrity that allows for growth, improvement, and lasting impact.

Embracing ordinary strengths means acknowledging the value in being reliable, consistent, and dedicated. It means finding pride in the small accomplishments, the daily routines, and the unglamorous tasks that make up the fabric of our lives. It means understanding that true power is not always loud, flashy, or extraordinary—sometimes, it's quiet, steady, and unassuming.

So, let us embrace the hidden power of mediocrity and recognize the strength that lies within the ordinary. Let us celebrate the unspectacular achievements, the minor victories, and the simple joys that make up our everyday lives. In doing so, we can find fulfillment, purpose, and meaning in the *seemingly* mundane—and unlock the true potential that lies within us all.

The Power within the Ordinary

Your mediocrity is a cloak that hides your brilliance, for in your ordinary existence lies an extraordinary power—the power of authenticity, of humility, of genuine human connection. You are the reminder that imperfection is not something to be ashamed of, but a testament to our shared humanity. Your ability to embrace your flaws and celebrate your quirks is a gift to us all, a beacon of light in a world that constantly demands perfection.

You may see yourself as mediocre, but to those who know you, you are anything but. Your presence brings comfort, laughter, and genuine connection to those around you. You are a source of inspiration, a reminder that it is okay to be exactly who you are, without pretense or embellishment.

So stand tall, dear friend, and know that you are a gift to the world. Embrace your ordinariness with pride, for in doing so, you shine a light on the beauty of simply being you. Your voice may be quiet, but it speaks volumes to those who are willing to listen.

You are extraordinary in your mediocrity, and that, my dear friend, is a truly remarkable gift.

Keep being you, for the world is a better place because of your authentic presence.

Therapeutic Summary

In this chapter, Laura talks about experiencing being bullied as a teen as a result of some physical issues she was experiencing at the time. This bullying led to her isolating herself at times and thoughts of self-harm, although she didn't take it to that level. Some people in Laura's situation may not only have thoughts of self-harm, but they may actually engage in self-harm, have suicidal ideation, or attempt suicide. Depression and anxiety can often accompany being bullied.

Resources

- Suicide & Crisis Lifeline — Dia/Text 988 — 988lifeline.org
- Crisis Text Line for Bullying — Text HOME to 741741 — crisistextline.org
- Stop Bullying Now — stopbullying.gov
- Counselor/Therapist -psychologytoday.com

The Power within the Ordinary

As Laura's journey with Coloradough Pizza draws to a bittersweet conclusion, she takes a moment to reflect on the profound impact the experience has had on her life. Grateful for the lessons learned, the doors opened, and the meaningful relationships formed during her time with the pizzeria, Laura fondly cherishes the memories and growth that have shaped her along the way.

While bidding farewell to Coloradough Pizza marks the end of one chapter, Laura's commitment to serving her community, particularly veterans, remains steadfast. With a deep sense of appreciation for those who have served their country, Laura is determined to continue her philanthropic efforts through acts of service and charity work.

Embracing the opportunities that lie ahead, Laura looks forward to channeling her passion for giving back into new endeavors that will further enrich the lives of others. With a heart full of gratitude for the past and a spirit brimming with optimism for the future, Laura is poised to embark on the next phase of her journey, carrying with her the enduring values of compassion, generosity, and service to others.

Keep Up with Laura

https://linktr.ee/laurafarley

Photo credits:
billymontanaimages.com
empire.edu/cosmetology-schools/colorado/aurora-denver

Follow our movement:

reigningresilientqueens.com

Breathe & Let It Be: Let Your Purpose Be Greater than Your Pain!

Lauren Jurkas

"I knew for certain that we never lose the people we love, even to death. They continue to participate in every act, thought, and decision we make! Their love leaves an indelible imprint in our memories." —Leo Buscaglia

Have you ever asked yourself, "Why me?"

I have.

Have you ever felt like a failure?

I have.

Have you ever believed that a mother's love is enough to keep her children safe?

I have.

Have you ever forgotten how to laugh?

I have.

Know that you are so much more than what you have experienced in your life. You are not what other people say you are. Unless someone has walked your personal journey, they don't have the authority to judge you or your choices. Everyone processes their difficulties in life differently, and that's okay. Ignore their unsolicited advice and their opinions about you.

I truly believed with all my heart that when I married the love of my life, Tony, and God blessed us with our two baby boys, we would be eternally happy for the rest of our lives.

Where Do I Begin?

Please join me as I revisit our family life in our younger years.

I was working as a restaurant manager at the Alexandria Steakhouse at the Empress Casino. One night, I received a call that shook me to my core. It was my husband, Tony, in a distressed voice forewarning me that when our boys, Tony Jr., seventeen, and Casey, twelve, arrived home, our house was on fire. When I hung up the phone, I was in shock and feeling numb. It felt like I was having an out-of-body experience. It was urgent that I regain my composure, so I asked my bartender to please drive me home because I was in no state of mind to get behind the wheel.

As we approached the highway on-ramp, the evening sky was blazing from the flames of our home ten miles away. At that exact moment, reality began to flood my brain, and I took a deep breath. I instantly went into Mom mode. When I arrived home, there were fire engines and emergency vehicles surrounding our home. Our entire neighborhood was gathered in the cul-de-sac directly in front of our home. I was so relieved to see my family and to hug my sweet boys and my husband. My boys had tried to hose down the fire when they arrived home, to no avail, but they were able to coax our dog, Taxi, to safety. Tony and Casey were our heroes that night! As the firefighters were tapping into several fire hydrants, they quickly discovered that every hydrant was dry. With urgency, they contacted several departments in the surrounding counties to truck in water. Unfortunately for us, it was too late. As the house burned, it became a five-alarm fire with no hope of saving our home. We, as a family, lost 99 percent of everything that we owned and had worked for.

I believe that when we search really hard during difficult times, we can find humorous moments. When I arrived home, the men were in "Big Boy's Toys" mode. What do I mean by that, you may ask? My husband and a few of the guys were hastily removing Tony Sr.'s Harley and Tony Jr.'s hockey goalie equipment from our garage. Did any of them ask Mama what she may want removed? Nope. And that's okay. Life goes on!

Our family life and dynamics were changed forever on that day in 2000. We had no choice but to rebuild our house from the ground up. This was an extremely humbling season for the Jurkas family. We relocated into a rental condo in Casey's school district to permit him to complete eighth grade with his classmates. You may ask why this was so humbling for us? Allow me to share with you that when we woke up displaced the following morning, not one of us had a toothbrush or a pair of underwear. This was the first time that the Jurkas family had no choice but to ask for love, support, and provisions. Please understand that we were never comfortable asking anyone for anything, but God overruled us and said it is time.

Know that God's timing is perfect regardless of your lack of understanding at that moment. When you open your heart and ask God for grace, the floodgates open wide. I can't begin to express the generosity that we were blessed with. Family, friends, and coworkers stepped up in every way. They delivered large storage bins filled to the top with every necessity that each family member didn't even realize they needed. These bins were filled with love and compassion. Always believe and claim what you are truly worthy of. Know you deserve love, my friends! Be conscious of the people who God places in your life in every season.

"Therefore do not be anxious, saying "What shall we eat?" or "What shall we drink?" or "What shall we wear?" For the gentiles seek after all these things, and your Heavenly Father knows that you need them all." —Matthew 6:31-32

In 2001, many things changed as we transitioned into our next chapter of life. We sold our house and built a new one in another town after Tony Jr. graduated from high school. My mom, Dorothy, had been diagnosed with dementia in 2000, and God took her home on June 21, 2001. Casey began his freshman year in a new high school. As you may imagine, I was quite concerned about whether or how he would adjust to his new school, teachers, and classmates. Casey had always had a difficult time adjusting to changes in his life.

Tony Jr. was working for a crane service company after graduating. He made the decision to step out on his own and get his own condo approximately forty-five miles away from us. It was time for Tony to fly, but I'm not sure our family was prepared for him to leave us.

One of our sons' favorite people on the planet was their Aunt Nancy. Aunt Nancy was diagnosed with breast cancer, and she lost her battle at age forty-seven in 2005. Nancy and I worked together in the same industry for years, and she was like a sister to me. How would I know that God was preparing me for something unimaginable in my future when God took Nancy home? I was also one of Nancy's caregivers, and when she died, it shook me to my core. In case you haven't figured out the pattern, I am an empath. We had to navigate how to move forward without Nancy in our lives. I was grateful that she was no longer suffering. She was finally at peace. The following Bible verse describes Nancy perfectly.

Ecclesiastes 3:4-5: "A time to cry and a time to laugh. A time to grieve and a time to dance. A time to scatter stones and a time to gather stones. A time to embrace and a time to turn away."

The day began like any other typical Easter Sunday in 2006. I had invited Tony Jr. and his girlfriend to join us for Easter dinner. He had confirmed that they would be there. I was anxiously looking forward to seeing them because Tony Jr. had a heavy work schedule, and he didn't get much time off. Tony Jr. and Casey were always the life of the party. We loved their energy and sense of humor. The week prior to Easter, I had severe stomach pains, which I believed were my maternal instincts kicking in. I shared what I was feeling with my husband and explained that I believed it was connected with our son, Tony Jr. I'm sure that he thought I was being overdramatic or maybe a little crazy. I had no idea why I was experiencing these pains. One thing that I knew for sure was that something wasn't right with Tony Jr. That was when I knew it was time to get on my knees and pray for him and his well-being. I always know that God is listening.

On Easter morning, Tony Sr. and I began prepping and cooking our dinner. We were having a great day. After all, it was Easter. As it got closer to dinner time, Tony Jr. had not arrived or called to check in with us. I truly wanted to believe that they were just running late. In my gut and in my heart and soul, I knew, as his mom, that something was very wrong. Tony, Casey, and I sat down at the table to eat dinner with two empty chairs! When we finished dinner and cleaned up, it was time to go to bed.

When we woke up Monday morning, April 17, 2006, there was no call or voicemail from Tony. My husband went to work, and Casey went to school. As any mom would do, I continued to try to reach Tony. I was incredibly worried about him. The day ended, and we still had not received any communication from him. It was now approximately ten p.m. and we decided to go to bed. I was emotionally drained.

My husband fell asleep immediately, but I was still awake when our doorbell began to ring repeatedly and loudly at approximately 10:30 p.m. Tony woke up, and I leaned over and said, "Don't worry, I'll go downstairs and answer the door." As I raced down the stairs, I was fixated on the front door where I saw two police officers in uniform. As I fearfully opened the front door, I thought, *What in the world is happening?* I wasn't ready to acknowledge the reality I was about to face. The officers asked me if my name was Lauren Jurkas and if I had a son, Michael Anthony Jurkas, who is twenty-three years old and lives in Naperville, Illinois. Tony had gotten out of bed and ran downstairs to see what was happening. By this time, I praised God that Tony was by my side. Feeling a bit numb, I answered yes to their questions.

At that moment, they replied that our son was found dead. I thought to myself, *That's not possible! There must be some kind of a mistake. Not my son! Maybe someone else's son but not our son.*

Instantly, I screamed at the top of my lungs, "NO!" and fell to my knees on the floor in disbelief and shock. I screamed in a piercing cry, "Oh my God! Oh my God! Oh my God!" The police officers offered to remain in our home to explain to Casey when he returned home that they had found his brother dead. We will be forever grateful for their kindness and compassion. I was begging God not to leave my side. I needed him desperately now. Tony and the officers escaped quietly into our kitchen to have a private conversation. When Tony returned, he shared with me that our beautiful son Tony died by suicide on Easter Sunday. Twenty-four hours later, a couple found Tony Jr.'s body in his condo storage area.

Now it was about midnight, and we called several family members and friends to share our horrific news about our oldest son. Hours later, so many loved ones showed up on our doorstep to show their love, compassion, and support for our family. We felt so blessed to have them in our lives at that exact moment. I felt like I was having an out-of-body experience. I could hear a great deal of noise and chatter, but I didn't feel present. Some even showed up with wine to toast our beautiful son Tony's life, which was comforting to all of us. You see, many of them had watched Tony grow up from a baby to a young man. I thought to myself, *Where do we go from here?* Our family and world as we knew it was broken wide open and was changed forever. I knew in my heart and soul that my family was destroyed that night and that we would never really heal. Why? Because we lost our son and Casey lost his only sibling to suicide. As you know, with death by suicide, there is always shame and guilt to process, as there was for all of us.

Let's talk about my faith in God for a minute. God was my only salvation at this exact moment, while I was trying to take a breath and process. He was and is my salvation always, under every circumstance. He told me that I needed to shift my focus from worrying about myself to saving and protecting my family immediately. He told me that we had many battles ahead of us that we needed to fight through as a family. He told me that I needed to take the lead. I also made a promise to God that night that I would never allow another person on this earth to feel so alone, or that they don't deserve to be loved for any reason.

When everyone went home, and I finally was able to go to bed at about three o'clock in the morning, my mind was racing like a machine. When my head hit the pillow, my first thought was, *Dear God, I need you now! Please help me think of a theme for our son's services because I don't want Casey or any of Tony Jr.'s friends to ask themselves why they didn't see any signs…*

When I opened my eyes at seven a.m., my new reality hit me like a ton of bricks. My son Tony was dead! This was my testimony from God! The first words that were dancing in my head when I woke up were, *Let it be*. I knew immediately that was God's answer to my question. That gave me a sense of peace, and I felt a calmness wash over my entire body. I thought none of us were really Beatles fans. We were more into the Rolling Stones and Motown, and Tony was into Dave Matthews. I'm sure that you have figured out what our new family anthem is.

Let it Be! You are welcome to borrow it. It is a little bittersweet, but beautiful. The lyrics made sense to me. "When I find myself in times of trouble, Mother Mary comes to me, speaking words of wisdom Let it Be … Let it Be!" This was a reminder from God to me to not search for answers to unanswerable questions. I created a "Let it Be" Facebook group for women and men to help them with their healing process through faith.

Another word that I couldn't stop thinking about was the word Breathe. God placed those words on my heart eighteen years ago, and they still calm me to this day. I had to practice what I preached about breathing when our son Casey spiraled into opioids years after his brother's death. I hit my knees in prayer, begging God to please give me the courage and strength to move on if he was going to take Casey home. We, as parents, did everything in our power to help Casey. His dad and I never gave up on him! My prayers were finally answered when Casey made the decision that it wasn't the life that he wanted for his future. As of today, Casey has been opioid-free for almost six years. Opioid addiction affects more than sixteen million people worldwide and more than 2.1 million in the USA.

When you lose a loved one, or you lose control of a situation, human instinct can sometimes be to hold your breath. Most times we don't even realize that we are holding our breath. The word breathe always reminds me to calm myself, and then I will be okay. I had to remind myself not to let my emotions take control of my mind and my body. It's not always an easy thing to do but practicing this will help you to center your thoughts.

Thankfully, there was some humor as well as the deep breathing. When I was gathering clothes for Tony that the funeral director had requested, I went upstairs to grab one more pair of Tony Sr.'s designer socks for the last time. You see, Tony Jr. would borrow (confiscate) Tony's designer clothes continuously. As I walked down the stairs, I looked up and laughed while saying, "You got him one more time, T." Another one was when I lost count of how many hams were delivered to our family. We got to the point where we could barely answer the door because we already knew that we were being gifted with yet another ham!

Today, I still ask myself, *Why didn't Tony Jr. know how much he was loved?* Tony Jr. was liked by everyone. He had a lucrative career as a diesel mechanic. He had a loving girlfriend, great family, and a loyal circle of friends from high school. He was quite handsome, very intelligent, and had an infectious smile. There were 3,000 guests at his wake, and he sold out five floral shops.

In closing, I want to remind you to never lose your faith! Know that everyone carries a story with them, and one we may know nothing about. Accept love and share your love. Breathe and keep your heart open through the process. Always check in on family and friends. Know that you are never alone. Be kind, and Let It Be!

Therapeutic Summary

In this chapter, Lauren experienced a great deal of loss from losing their home in a fire and then the death of her oldest son. These types of loss can result in grief, depression, anxiety, and, for some, trauma. In regard to losing a child to suicide, Lauren mentioned the guilt and shame that can be felt. Parents, family members, and friends can often blame themselves for not knowing their loved one is suicidal; however, in most cases of completed suicide, no one is aware of how their loved one is actually feeling or that anything is wrong. The majority of completed suicides do not give any indication of what they are thinking of or planning on doing, which comes as a shock to their loved ones. After the death of her oldest, Lauren's youngest developed an opioid addiction. Opioid addiction is an epidemic in America and includes addiction to legal and illegal drugs such: Xanax, painkillers, heroin, and fentanyl. While Lauren never states she directly experienced depression or anxiety around her grief, it is common to see these issues manifest from such a loss. Something that is important to keep in mind as a person navigates grief and loss is that there is no right or wrong way to process, there is no right or wrong amount of time, and it's a cycle, not a straight line. After a loss, a person may fluctuate between the various stages of grief for days, weeks, months, and even years. The important thing to keep in mind is that we don't want to stay at any of the stages outside of acceptance for too long. Finding oneself in any stage of grief for a prolonged period of time can indicate the presence of prolonged grief, which requires therapeutic intervention.

Resources

- American Foundation for Suicide Prevention — afsp.org
- The Compassionate Friends — compassionatefriends.org
- Let it Be Healing Facebook Group — https://www.facebook.com/groups/190378788292862
- Opioid Resources — victoriasvoice.foundation
- Grief & Loss Stages — healgrief.org

THANK YOU FOR TAKING THE TIME to get to know me! My name is Lauren Jurkas, and I have co-authored two books, volunteered, and fundraised for the American Foundation for Suicide Prevention, and launched an Illinois chapter for The Compassionate Friends support group for anyone who has lost a child, sibling, or grandchild at any age for any reason. My career was in hospitality management, and for the last ten years I have been managing my personal independent Mary Kay Cosmetics Business.

I profoundly believe that my purpose in life is to connect people as well as making everyone feel loved and to never settle for less than they deserve. Through Mary Kay, my goal is to make my clients feel important and to know their self-worth. I hope that they see their beauty through my eyes.

My hope for you while reading my chapter is for you to believe that we all can choose to learn lessons and flourish from our experiences in our lives!

Keep Up with Lauren

https://linktr.ee/queenlj55

Photo credits:
d20photography.com
empire.edu/cosmetology-schools/colorado/aurora-denver

Follow our movement:

reigningresilientqueens.com

Finding My Note: A Story of Resilience and Redemption

Marta Spirk

> "If I can make it there, I can make it anywhere."
> —"New York, New York" by Frank Sinatra

EVERY SUNDAY AFTERNOON, I remember my dad used to play old classics at around lunchtime: Frank Sinatra, Nat King Cole, the Beatles, Bee Gees, and ABBA. Growing up in Brazil, we had so much influence from American and British music and movies. I'm very grateful my parents exposed me to it all, as it had such a big impact on my teenage and adult years, so much so that I started my performing career back at home.

I've lost count of all the childhood pictures and videos of me singing with a makeshift microphone in hand. And every single one of my family members can attest that I would parade around the house from room to room carrying a big boombox and demanding everyone stop and watch me perform.

In my early teens, I finally convinced my mom to put me in voice and piano lessons. I was happy to show my progress, singing and playing in her church as I got more comfortable. For a while, I thought I'd never have to go to college if I followed the path of ministry. I thought I could make a living speaking and singing, but my dad had other plans. So, I picked the closest career I could to mastering musical sounds—learning and teaching languages. I was very good at them, and I now see that it had a lot to do with my ear for music. I ended up getting a degree in Translation in Portuguese, English, and French. By then, music had taken a backseat to pursuing love. I met my husband at a church conference in Tulsa, Oklahoma, and after five years of long-distance dating, we got married, and I moved to the US.

As I adjusted to the married, grown-up life away from my family and everything I had ever known, I completed a master's in applied linguistics at the University of Colorado Denver. Music remained a side passion, a hobby. Every now and again, it would resurface and I'd entertain the idea of being a serious singer or musician. I auditioned to sing the national anthem at a commencement ceremony and also for "The Voice" television show in Brazil. The rejections confirmed it wasn't my path or at least that it was definitely not my time.

The next step was starting a family. Much to my surprise, about eighteen months into trying to conceive, I learned I was pregnant with triplets. Nothing could have ever prepared me for this news. As happy and grateful as I was, I was also very scared—not only health wise, but future wise. Having triplets, in many ways, confirmed to me that I'd never get to do so many things I had dreamed of doing, like becoming a professional singer and performer. I remember a very distinct moment while spending time with my babies when I felt this disappointing realization set in.

I was sitting in our messy living room surrounded by babies and their toys watching, "So You Think You Can Dance," a dance competition show, where young dancers from all over the US audition and showcase their skills. As I saw those beautiful girls perform, I remember thinking, *That could have been me*. Even though my dream wasn't to pursue dance, I grieved then, being thirty years old and far past the point where I could compete, let alone become a performer.

It was around that time I decided that while I may not follow a musical path, I could still make something out of myself beyond motherhood. Back in 2016, I started my own coaching business as I understood there were so many possibilities to make money with an online business.

I got some life coaching certifications and began offering programs online, serving clients, and learning how to monetize the skills I'd acquired. With time, I learned it was important to become known for my expertise and establish myself as an expert in my field. So, I began a media mentoring course that encouraged me to find more speaking opportunities and exposure.

In 2019, I landed my very first TV segment in the local news and went on to become a regularly featured expert on the show. I also reconnected with my *alma mater* and did my first keynote presentation. I would pitch to and accept pretty much anything that got me in front of an audience. That was when I heard about a national anthem contest on the local country radio station, and I didn't think twice about entering.

Soon, my whole family and friends, plus all the social media following I had built in the previous three years, were involved in voting for me to win the competition. On January 16th, 2020, I got to sing the national anthem at a professional rodeo in front of around 10,000 people. What a rush that was! The performance bug had officially bitten me, and I wasn't going to let it go this time.

That singing opportunity opened doors to more national anthem performances, which encouraged me to take up voice lessons again. Two decades later, I was being coached to sing once more, and it felt so right. My coach,

Melissa Cartwright, also helped with songwriting. I felt compelled to write my own music, which, in my mind, would be private songs for my coaching clients.

Not only have I professionally produced these original songs in a studio, but I have also released a few singles on major music streaming platforms. As I write this, in 2024, I have performed the national anthem in front of up to 50,000 people for several professional sports teams, sharing courts and fields with top celebrity athletes, and was also invited to sing the theme song for this collaboration book.

By now, you may be asking, But, Marta, how did you go from grieving a life that never was, holding triplet babies, to establishing yourself as a professional singer in your late thirties?

I continued to entertain the dreams and desires that seemed crazy and impossible until they became very much possible and real. And I'm here to tell you that you can do this, too. Looking back, there were specific steps I took through the years that led me to standing here. I want to share them with you.

Entertain It

As you read through my story, your brain may have brought back memories about desires you have had and have not allowed yourself to pursue. What are they? And in case nothing has resurfaced yet, I encourage you to take some time to reflect and see what comes up.

As a coach, I have facilitated breakthroughs for so many women in the pursuit of their dreams. It all started, however, because I took the time to go through several coaching programs and introspective exercises myself. I can absolutely attest to the benefits of continuously prompting yourself with a journaling practice. It's incredible how many insights you can have through self-discovery.

This is why my number one advice to turn a crazy desire into reality is to first figure out what crazy ideas you have. In other words, entertain your desires by giving them thought. Even if it seems unfeasible, resist your brain's urge to dismiss it.

Here are some questions you can journal on:

- What is something you dreamed of doing, having, or being as a child?
- Do you have a hobby you wish you had more time to pursue?
- If time, money, or any other obstacle wasn't an issue, what would you do?

Perform It

Our brains are wired to protect us from imminent threats. And if you overrule its first protection mechanism by entertaining your dreams with your thoughts, there is yet another hurdle to overcome: fear of taking action.

If your brain can't keep you from dreaming, it will try its best to make sure you don't take action to make your dreams come true. So many people stop at this stage. I can't emphasize it enough—you *must* take action.

The problem is that it takes so much courage to act. When we don't see results right away or experience any resistance, disappointment or rejection, our brains come in yet again and remind us, "See, it's not safe. Go back to where you were."

I hope you remember my words and *keep going*!

So many of my clients, as they began journaling and entertaining their dreams, have gathered the strength to take action by going back to painting or admitting to themselves they've always wanted to sing and join a choir.

Here are some ideas to get you moving after you entertain your crazy dreams:

- Do you know anyone who is doing what you want to do? Make a list and reach out to at least one of them to learn more.

- Is there a support group or networking community that you could visit or join to help you perform your dream?
- Are there classes you can enroll in to learn more about or refine your skill in this area?

Keep At It

Once you bypass your fear of dreaming and taking action, the next gatekeeper in your brain is the temptation to overthink and give up. I guarantee your mind will go a hundred miles per hour trying to formulate the perfect ten-year plan to make your crazy dream come true and simultaneously give you a hundred reasons why it won't work out, or even if it does, any progress will be a fluke.

This is when it's vital for you to keep going and, most importantly, have fun! Forget about time. In fact, lose track of time and relish the joy of pursuing your dream. Chances are, performing actions related to your dreams will make you feel the most authentic to yourself (that's why it's so scary!), so you have to focus on the positive. Otherwise, you will rationalize it away and throw in the towel.

Here are some encouraging suggestions when you feel like giving up:

- In writing, describe in as much detail as possible how you feel when you are performing actions related to your dreams.
- Whenever you feel discouraged, read those pages or evoke those feelings to remind yourself *why* you are pursuing this dream.
- Surround yourself with people who support your dreams, and reach out to them when you feel discouraged so they can lift you up.

While you may not have been born in another country and found yourself holding triplet babies like me, I believe you have a seed inside of you that can be nurtured by this message of hope.

It is absolutely not too late to unlock your gifts, find your voice, and use it to empower the world. It starts with empowering yourself. I know you can do it.

Therapeutic Summary

In this chapter, Marta discusses grieving for a period of time the life she envisioned for herself but had not come to pass yet. Grief can be experienced around a number of different situations and circumstances. People most often associate grief with death, however, grief can be experienced during life transitions such as graduating high school or college, leaving one career for a new career or one job for another job, leaving a familial or romantic relationship, moving away from an area, or having a vision of a future that hasn't been attained. It is not uncommon to see grief manifest into depression, as explained in other chapters in this book.

Resources

- Coaching by Marta Spirk — martaspirk.com
- Counseling/Therapy — psychologytoday.com

BORN IN BRAZIL WITH A LOVE OF MUSIC, Marta Spirk's journey is a testament to the power of never giving up on dreams. From a young age, music was undeniably part of her, but life had other plans. Marta's linguistic prowess led her to a career in languages, and love took her to the United States after marrying her American husband.

Blessed with the arrival of triplets, Marta embraced the adventure of motherhood while never losing sight of her own identity. With a voice that refused to be silenced, she fearlessly pursued coaching and media mentoring, seizing every chance to let her talent shine. Her crowning moment came when she won a national anthem singing contest, a reminder that her musical dreams were destined for greatness.

Determined to make her mark, Marta dove headfirst into honing her craft as an adult. Voice lessons and songwriting became her passion, and she emerged as a force to be reckoned with. Today, Marta's soulful performances and infectious spirit captivate audiences, serving as a beautiful reminder that it's never too late to become the star of your own story.

Keep Up with Marta

martaspirk.com

Photo credits:
d20photography.com
empire.edu/cosmetology-schools/colorado/aurora-denver

Follow our movement:

reigningresilientqueens.com

Hiding in Plain Sight: A Quest to Be Seen

Shantelle Bridges

"You were a great kid, Shantelle. Until you turned about ten, then something changed." We were gathered at my parents' house for family dinner, reminiscing. As siblings do, bickering over who was the best child. But the moment I heard my mother say those words, I felt sick to my stomach. She had no idea why everything changed. She could not see what I had spent decades concealing. Soon, she would see the hurt that was shouting from my soul to *"be seen."*

"I see you." These three words have freed women right before my eyes. I've sat with dozens of women aching to hear the words they've never been offered and watching as the power of being seen does its work. I've walked through seasons in my life that have taught me the impact of not being seen and not having support.

I passionately enter every conversation to see how I can refresh and support the woman on the other side of the table. When women hear, "I see you, even in your struggle." And they hear the words, "You are not alone," space is created for healing. When women are offered words of encouragement that are drenched in compassion, the shame they've held through hiding is silenced and they are empowered to grow.

I wonder how different it would have been if someone had asked me the questions I longed to have asked. "Shantelle, something is different. Is there anything going on?" I know that if someone had seen *my behaviors as the symptom and not the root, with compassion instead of discipline or judgment, things would have been different for me.* I think back to my ten-year-old self and how she longed to hear the words that she was seen, acknowledged, and supported through it all.

Perhaps life would have been different for me if I had heard those words as a pregnant teen riddled with shame. The impact of those words could have comforted me when I lost my baby at twenty, acknowledging my grief and easing my pain. I think back to how these words might have been a glimmer of hope as I walked through divorce with very little support. Every traumatic event replays in my mind, reminding me of what happens when we lack the two things we need the most: *to be seen and supported.*

The Story Written in Hiding

We all tell ourselves stories. These stories are shaped by what happened to us. We hold them in our bones as we walk through life. From a young age, my story has centered around the ache of wanting to be seen and the belief system that *I could only survive by hiding* my truth.

My mother used to work for a local group home. Some of the boys weren't in contact with their families and were left there during the holidays.

One year, my parents decided to be a blessing and bring one of the sixteen-year-old boys' home so he wouldn't be alone. It was Christmas break, and we had a lot of time on our hands and not enough to do. One day, we decided to cure our boredom and venture out and about the neighborhood, he on foot, me on my bike. As we traveled, my ten-year-old self-trailing behind the sixteen-year-old leading the way, he pulled into an empty school. I got off my bike with trust and an innocence I unknowingly would be robbed of. He led me there with intentions I would have never imagined he had. We walked a bit toward a covered tunnel, and my young, trusting mind kept me from perceiving the danger in the moment.

Alone and unprotected, he molested me there. As I wept, he stood over me, asserting the same power he wielded to take advantage of me, and insisted I gather myself before we head back. With an eerie tone he looked me in the eyes and said, *"If you tell your parents, I will kill them."* I believed him. Because why wouldn't I? To me, a boy who could do what was done in that tunnel was capable of other dark deeds.

I rode back, broken and afraid, knowing I would be returning to a dynamic that would never be the same. What was I supposed to do? I was told that my parents, the ones who had always protected me, couldn't know what happened to me. I was desperate for them to see the hurt I was carrying but too afraid to expose the truth out of fear that it would be detrimental to all of us. I was walking around with a secret and emotions bigger than my ten-year-old self. I wanted someone, anyone, to see what I was concealing. I was forced to make the choice to live a life of hiding.

I remember lying on the couch, stuck in the memory of what had happened. I can't help but acknowledge how my mother noticed but still didn't see. She knew something was wrong but, perhaps, she didn't know how to ask the questions that would dig deeper. *A life lesson for us all. To see others, we must be willing to look deeper.* Before this traumatic event, I was an honest and trusting little girl, loved and adored by her amazing parents.

After the traumatic event, I became who I believed I needed to be to cope with the trauma I couldn't disclose. I became—a liar. Suddenly, withholding the truth was the only way to protect myself. Even though I was hiding to stay safe, deep inside, I was pleading. *Hey, look at me, look at me, look at me! Can someone see me? Can someone acknowledge me?* It wasn't until I was thirty-five that the internal voice finally escaped my lips, and I told my parents what happened.

A few weeks before I decided to have this hard conversation with my parents, we were at their house, and my siblings and I were arguing about who was the best child. I would always say it was me. Even though I was a teen mom, I really wasn't much of a rebel. I didn't do drugs or alcohol, and rarely got in trouble for anything except talking too much, which would not surprise anyone who knows me.

Then that statement, "I agree with that, Shantelle, until you turned about ten years old …" my mom interjected. When she said those words, I knew it was time seek the inward healing through my faith, the Bible, and the *God who sees all, El Roi, Genesis 16:13*. It was the first time I had heard them refer to the moment I believed had gone unnoticed all these years. I realized that the secret I had been hiding did not just impact me. The way I carried the pain, even in secret, was seen in a way I never realized. I thought I was good at tucking that moment away, but all along, the people in my life were witnessing the rotten fruit of the aftermath.

No matter how good I thought I was at hiding what had happened, my choices were an attempt to get someone to notice me. Trauma has a way of sticking to us. After trauma is experienced, the aftermath of actions, not the root, is noticed by most first. Though I felt a sense of validation that though my parents were able to see the impact of what happened to me, I couldn't receive the freedom on the other side of them, seeing the seed that was planted and not just the bad fruit it bore.

Uprooting the Seeds of Being Unseen

Resilience is more than bouncing back from the painful things we experience in life. It is, at times, the decision to uproot what the seeds of our past have produced. My past produced weeds, and it was time to uproot what had grown by finally telling the truth. There was a sermon I heard many years after this part of my story, where my pastor spoke of how seeds ensure the continuation of a pattern. It made me think of how I had lived almost twenty-five years trapped in a pattern that began when that ten-year-old girl was abused. The seed that was planted at that traumatic moment created a pattern where I made choices from my wounds instead of from a place of healing.

When I decided it was time to tell my parents what had happened to me, it was because I knew God was saying, "*It's time to pull this root up from the ground. They need to know what was done.*" So, I called them and told them I wanted to come over so we could talk. I was terrified that the guilt I had carried all those years would be transferred to them. But the fear of living one more day trapped in the cycle of hiding outweighed whatever outcome I would encounter with this conversation.

I arrived at their house, full of nerves and a small bit of hope that this moment would finally heal me. I would be lying if I did not admit that I carried a certain expectation in my heart as I walked into the house and sat down to speak. Then I began to tell them my story as if I was experiencing it now. "It happened that horrible day in December …" Once I finished, I can't remember who spoke first, but I remember what was said. "Well, Shantelle," my mother begins, "thank you for telling us. This makes me respect you. I have always respected you, but this makes me think even more highly of you that you had this happen in your life and have been able to continue your life this way."

Then my dad says, "This is good to know. I thought your behavior was because of me and how I was living back then. I have always thought that your challenges resulted from the fact of something I did or didn't do."

Though I felt relieved that this secret was now out in the open, I was devastated by their response. The main reason I never told them was because

I thought they would be devastated. Now, *where do I find my healing?* It would be in Jesus, my heavenly Father, and those He would send to me to "see me."

I was never afraid that they wouldn't believe me. I was afraid that they would be riddled with guilt. They still didn't see what I needed them to see. Therefore, they couldn't say what my heart needed to hear. No one said, "I'm sorry" or "That shouldn't have happened to you." They reacted to what I said, but no one said anything to the little girl who had gone through it all.

I left that day wrecked. I sat in my car crying and angry. I thought to myself, *how did they still not see the impact?* Though they both said things like, "I'm proud of you" and "We love you," their words fell short. My pain needed the comfort of hearing, "I see you! I acknowledge you! I'm sorry that happened to you." The expectation I had in my heart was for my parents to validate my pain in a *specific way*. I especially longed for my mother to look back at that time and see what my ten-year-old self couldn't say.

I wanted her to look past the bad behavior and see the girl who had to be acting out for a reason. I wanted her to dig deeper for that reason. I was waiting for her validation in a way that was stalling my healing. My parents showed up to my pain the way they knew how.

I had to decide to accept that and continue forward. To receive how they could show up and to take responsibility for my own healing, by allowing the God who loved me and wanted to heal me, to do only what He could do.

Because I understand the significance of what I needed from my mother and the difference I believe that may have made in my life, I walked through mothering my children with a deliberate mindset. My mother is one of the most amazing people I know, and my greatest example of love. Yet, in this broken place, I couldn't receive what I needed from her. As a mother, it has always been essential for me to see my children despite everything.

No matter what I was going through, whether I was struggling with how to pay our bills or walking through my divorce, my desire was to always create space for my children to be seen. There were many nights when my girls were young that they would sit on my bed, and I would listen to them tell the story of my divorce and how it affected them. I would lean in as if to say, *"Let me hear. Let me see. Let me be there."*

You can't control the way people can show up to your pain. We all respond based on the emotional toolbox we possess. You can push past pain's stronghold. Choosing to validate and to be a woman who sees those who need you to help them as you desire continues your healing too. Having empathy for someone's pain is seeing them. When people are seen, they are strengthened to push through. We rarely want to talk about what happened to us, as much as we want to talk about how what happened affected us. In sharing, we step out of the lie that we must carry our stuff on our shoulders, and we see the beauty in letting God and people into our stories as another display of resilience.

Letting Ourselves Be Seen

At twenty-seven weeks pregnant, my water broke. My then-husband was in the military, and we were stationed in Germany. There were too many patients in the American hospital, so we were contracted out to the German hospital. Once we arrived, I was admitted to the hospital, where everyone was German and barely spoke English. Because of the language barrier, I felt like I was in the dark and rarely knew what was going on while I was there.

My husband would come to visit me every day, although the hospital was over an hour away, while he was also caring for our five-year-old son. In the wee hours of the morning on November 11th, 1991, I went into labor. I remember my nurse being a petite woman with bright red hair. She looked at me and said, "Okay, honey, we are going to have this baby." I knew then that I was going to have my son, Christopher Michael, and that he was going to die. The nurse with the red hair, I found out later, didn't exist. When I described her to the other staff members, there was no record of a red-headed nurse on staff. Believe what you may, but I know she was an angel sent by God to walk through this dark moment with me.

As I labored, knowing that my child would not make it earthside, I never once told anyone to call my husband. I knew he had our son, and I didn't want him to be bothered with this tragic moment; I would spare him this heartache. Looking back, I realize that my choice to be alone was tied to the story formed when I was a ten-year-old. "This is my tragedy. I don't want to impact anyone else. I am going to go through this alone."

I robbed my husband of a moment he needed for his grieving journey. I robbed myself of the comfort of being held while experiencing great loss. To be seen in life requires us to invite people in to bear witness to our pain and to see our humanity. It wasn't until I began the work of letting God pull up the roots from the seeds that were burrowed into the soil from my past that I realized *to be resilient doesn't mean to do life alone.*

There are seasons when you must truly walk alone, but there are also times when you shut people out because you believe resilience is a strength that stands alone. The truth is that resilience is a strength that is surrounded by others. It wasn't until my thirties I recognized this truth, as God continued to send mentors into my life. It was clear that I was not created to thrive by myself.

You are not created to thrive by yourself. I had spent years tethered to the lie that I could only survive in this world by hiding. Soon, I didn't just hide behind deceiving others; I hid behind the facade of having it all together.

Our resistance to community robs us of the very thing we need. Resilience is not resisting the desire to be surrounded by people who will see you at your lowest. To be resilient is to be surrounded. It's the decision to choose your tribe and create your village. It's the commitment to stay connected and remain vulnerable enough to be seen and humble enough to be supported, and to know that you are worthy of both.

Face the Hard

I've heard it said, and I've lived it to the truth: You don't know God is all you need until God is all you have. And strength is similar. You don't know strength until you've experienced the kind of thing that requires a certain kind of strength. But we do not receive this strength by denying the impact our past has had on us. For many years, I was in denial that the pain of my past was still lingering in my present. I thought that by presenting myself as a good, strong woman, I could prove that I wasn't affected by the things that happened to me.

When I became pregnant in my senior year of high school, I tried to cope with the shame by appearing to be strong. I watched as my dreams slipped through my hands, fault being my own. I struggled with the thought of being a disappointment to my parents. I thought pushing through would fix me, but I ended up jumping from one thing to the next with the same wounds. I thought marriage would fix me, but it only exposed the wounds I never dealt with. We can spend our whole lives running from the pain of our past, or we can *run toward it and find freedom that God desires to provide for us.*

I've spent a lot of time living in Colorado, home of the famous Rocky Mountains. Many people don't know that the western part of the state is composed of the rocky terrain of the mountains and the eastern part of the state is the Kansas Plains. Because of this unique landscape, Colorado is the only place where there are both bison and cows. Whenever there is a storm, cows sense it and begin running east to outrun the storm. Because cows are not as fast as they think and the storm eventually catches up to them, instead of outrunning the storm, they end up running with it.

Bison, on the other hand, will wait for the storm to cross over a ridge. Once it rolls over, bison will change direction and *run into the storm*. Because they face the storm and run at it, they can run through it. When we are seen and supported, we are empowered to be like the bison and run toward the storm to get through the storm. That is what resilient women do. They do the work of facing their pain, their battle, their struggle, and refuse to let the past become their identity. Resilient women don't spend their lives attaching their worth to being seen but experience the blessing of being surrounded by others who validate the pain that needs to heal.

You may have grown up with a definition of resilience that has not been proven true in your life. But freedom is on the other side of redefining what strength and resilience means to you. Strength is not the absence of weeping, and resilience is not the absence of pain. Resilience is choosing to say, "This hurts, but I will continue on." It's the strength to face the storm, knowing that the only way out is through. And once through, we may laugh as Proverbs 31:25 points out, "She is clothed with strength and dignity; and she laughs without fear of the future."

Therapeutic Summary

In this chapter, Shantelle lived through two traumatic events, being molested and giving birth to a child who had died. As a result of these events, Shantelle may have experienced PTSD, anxiety, depression, and grief. As a mother, losing your child at birth causes understandable grief, and being molested as a child can also cause grief around losing your innocence and having your youth stolen from you. For Shantelle, all she wanted was to be seen and to hear, "I'm sorry this happened to you." This is a desire so many of us have. To be seen. To be heard. To know someone cares.

Resources

- Celebrate Recovery — celebraterecovery.com
- Counseling/Therapy — psychologytoday.com
- Star Legacy Foundation — starlegacyfoundation.org

SHANTELLE BRIDGES has been a noteworthy community leader and activist, directing impactful programs in the nonprofit space for over twenty years. Her program success and advocacy have been featured in the *Colorado Springs Business Journal*. You may know her as a dynamic and influential motivational speaker who has dedicated her life to empowering individuals to unlock their full potential, overcome adversity, and live purposeful lives. Shantelle delivers transformational messages of hope and empowerment as she draws on her expertise as a life coach and extensive experience as a public educator. She intertwines her personal experiences and struggles, delivering dynamic talks that challenge attendees to break free from societal constraints and live authentically. Shantelle's focus on value, grace, and vision resonates with individuals from all walks of life. Whether she is addressing corporate leaders, entrepreneurs, students, or those simply seeking to become the best version of themselves, her message leaves a lasting impact, leading individuals toward a path of personal growth and success.

Keep Up with Shantelle

shantellebridges.com

Photo credits:
d20photography.com
empire.edu/cosmetology-schools/colorado/aurora-denver

Follow our movement:

reigningresilientqueens.com

There is Light in Every Day

Stacey Sanders

I HAD BEEN WAITING FOR an important phone call for about a week. It was a call that had a strong likelihood of changing my life forever. As such, I was anxious and jumped every time my phone rang. On the day the call came, I was in the middle of facilitating a writing workshop with some of the youth participants. We were ten days away from our first Poetry Jam. At 4:30 p.m. on May 10, 2018, the call came. I stepped out of the room to answer. The person on the other end of the phone said the words I was certain were coming but prayed would not be said. "It's what we thought. You have Parkinson's." Seven words that changed my life forever. I stood in the hallway of the Blair Caldwell Library in Denver trying to absorb what this meant. The first two questions I asked the physician's assistant were, "Will I be able to continue working?" and, "Will this kill me?" Her answers were yes and no. I thanked her for the call and told her I'd see her the following week at my already scheduled appointment. I was fifty-one years old.

Then I just stood there, leaning against the wall, looking at my phone for what seemed like an eternity. I took some deep breaths, put my phone in my pocket, and walked back into the room. The young people needed me to be in that room with them. Two people there knew I was waiting for that call and why. As I walked in, I nodded yes to both of them. Their faces quickly changed from anticipation to shock to concern. One gave me a hug. At that moment, I made a choice to be present for the young people. All of them were current and former youth in foster care, who were brave and sharing their stories through spoken word poetry. Their stories are painful and full of trauma, yet they are also full of hope and inspiration. They inspire me every day.

As the workshop wrapped up, my anxiety ramped up because I knew I had people to tell. I had endless questions about treatments and medications. I had to decide who to call first. *How do you tell people this kind of news?* After I said goodbye to all of our youth participants, I sat in my car for I don't know how long, contemplating my future and feeling very scared and alone.

The first symptom had occurred sometime in the summer of 2017. I noticed a small tremor in my left middle finger, and my hand would sometimes get stuck on the keyboard or would simply jump off the keyboard. I knew this wasn't normal, but I had no time to focus on what might be happening to me because 2017 was an incredibly difficult year for my family. We lost three family members within the span of seven months, and in the midst of all of that my mom had to have her gallbladder removed, and things did not go well right after the surgery. My mother became septic as soon as she was in recovery, and it took multiple doctors to save her life. Thus began weeks of hospitalization, emotional upheaval, and concern for my mother's long-term health.

Fortunately, my mother made it through that medical challenge, like she had so many others, and I found a way to return to my normal routines. I had not discussed with anyone that I was having tremors in my left hand. I chose to ignore it because I simply did not have the capacity or the desire to figure out what was happening to me. Somewhere in the back of my mind I knew that I was going to have to deal with this situation at some point. Toward the end of the year, I did share the tremor with two of my coworkers. They both agreed that it seemed odd and not normal.

In January 2018, I knew I had to go see my doctor. The tremor was increasing in my middle finger and my left hand didn't seem to be as strong as my right hand. My journey to the official diagnosis began in February 2018, first with my primary care physician and then with a neurologist. My neurology appointment started with a physician's assistant who took my history and examined me. She then brought in the doctor who repeated some of the exam, which included me walking up and down the hallway. The doctor told me that I needed a series of tests, starting with blood work, an MRI, and finally a dopamine transporter scan (DaTscan) test. He explained that the DaTscan is specifically for testing dopamine levels to diagnose Parkinson's disease.

The DaTscan took about six hours, easy enough physically but stressful knowing what they were looking for. When I received the call from the physicians' assistant, one question I asked was, "What led you to Parkinson's besides the tremor?" She responded that my left arm does not swing when I walk. I had no idea that my arm had stopped swinging. I would later learn that there are more than sixty symptoms tied to Parkinson's disease. It turns out that most people have symptoms for years before a diagnosis. Learning that answered a lot of questions for me because I did in fact have things happening to my body that I could not explain. One in particular is that my toes curl and become very painful. I thought it was only that I was wearing the wrong shoes. Nope, instead of just bad shoes, I had the fun of having a progressive neurological disorder. Lucky me!

I had told my two wonderful sisters, some coworkers, and some friends that I was being tested for Parkinson's disease. I decided to hold off telling my mom until I knew what I was dealing with. No need to worry her unnecessarily. So, as I sat in my car that day I received the diagnosis, I called my sister Marla first. She was surprised yet incredibly supportive, offering to go with me to the doctor for the first appointment. I then had to call my sister, Allison, who was with my mom at the time. I told her that I was sorry to leave this in a message. I honestly cannot remember if I made any other phone calls that night. I did send text messages to my friends and coworkers to let them know, but I told them I was not up for phone calls that night. In the text to my boss, I told her I would be at work the next day. She asked me if I was sure, and at that moment, I was convinced that work the next day was just what I needed.

I did not get much sleep that night and as such, I texted my boss and told her that I would not be in that day after all. My wonderful coworkers brought me my favorite comfort foods from a restaurant in Denver. They didn't ask if they could come over because they figured I would tell them no, and they were right. However, when I went to greet them outside, their hugs were very welcome, and the food did offer me comfort. It's important to remember that when people show up for you, you should let them, particularly if you are going through a difficult time. I will always be grateful for the kindness and compassion they showed me in that moment.

The hardest phone call of all was when I told my mom. I went over and over it in my head countless times so that I could find the right words to tell her. My sisters and I coordinated the time that I would call her. The plan was for me to text them when it was done so they could support her. I knew once I told my mom, I would not be able to give her the comfort that she would need because I was still very much dealing with the impact of the diagnosis.

I got my mom on the phone, and I said, "I have something difficult to tell you, and it's not going to be easy to hear. I'm going to say it, and then we can talk about it. I have Parkinson's disease." My mom has received a lot of difficult news in her lifetime, but none is as difficult as learning that one of her kids had a progressive neurological disorder. I gave her as much information as I could. She was shocked but supportive during our entire conversation. I told her the girls would be calling her soon. To this day, I do not know what kinds of conversations my mom and sisters had or how my mom coped with the news on that Friday afternoon. What I do know is that my mom and sisters have been loving and supportive throughout my Parkinson's journey.

My story does not begin or end with Parkinson's. I was born and raised in Colorado, the oldest of three girls. Our dad passed away in 1995 at the age of fifty-five from pulmonary hypertension. My sisters each married wonderful, kind men, and thanks to all of them, I am the aunt of four; one niece and three nephews. They are the absolute light and joy of my life. My family means everything to me, and I would truly be lost in this world without them.

My professional path has not been a straight line. I've changed careers three times, and that journey has led me to find work that fuels my soul and allows me to make an impact in the lives of others. I began my career working in the criminal justice system with adult felony offenders at a halfway house. After eight years of working in that field, I took a sharp right and fulfilled a secret dream I had of owning a flower shop. I worked in my shop for six years and loved providing beautiful floral arrangements for my customers. After I closed my shop due to the economy, I went into retail management for nearly eight years. When the company I worked for went out of business, I decided it was time for me to return to my roots of working in human services. It was then, in 2011, that I found my true calling, which is advocating for and working with youth in the foster care system.

When I began my career in child welfare, I had no idea that a few short years later, I would become the founder and executive director of my own nonprofit. On January 31, 2015, Elevating Connections was founded with a small but mighty group of people who became my board of directors. We work with siblings who have been separated from one another due to abuse and neglect in their home. We also work with older youth who have experienced foster care by giving them opportunities to speak their truth through the arts. I am very proud of the work we do, and I am so incredibly grateful for the team of people who have given their hearts, their time, and their money so we can provide quality programming for the young people we serve.

My work is my passion. It fills my heart and brings me great joy, especially when I am working directly with the kids and youth we serve. It is this work that has sustained me. It kept me motivated, along with my family and friends, to keep showing up and to keep the faith that obstacles like Parkinson's will not bring me down or stop me from living life on my terms. The youth I work with inspire me every day because of their determination and drive to build lives that allow them to find joy and purpose.

My faith and determination were further tested on March 13, 2021, when a fire caused me to lose most of what I owned and traumatized me like nothing else in my life, even Parkinson's. I live in a one-bedroom condominium on the second floor. The neighbor right below me started a fire in his fireplace and forgot to open the flue. When he did, it caused the fire to shoot out the back of his fireplace, and the building caught fire. I stood on the sidewalk and watched my home go up in flames. It was snowing heavily and was extremely cold. A kind neighbor brought me a blanket, and then I sat in an ambulance while the firefighters tried to save my home. Fortunately, no one was injured, and after four days I found my cat, Amelia, scared but safe.

Thus began a journey of dealing with the aftermath of my home, my safe place, having to be gutted and rebuilt in order for me to return home. Thanks to two of my dear friends, I was able to recover some of my belongings, most importantly items that make me feel closer to my dad.

I was faced with rebuilding my life. I spent the next nine months living at my mom's, working my full-time job, running my nonprofit, and trying to take care of myself because stress and anxiety exacerbated my Parkinson's symptoms. Those nine months were some of the most challenging of my life. I have had anxiety most of my adult life, and it was at an all-time high while my home was being rebuilt. My friends, family, and coworkers were kind and supportive throughout those nine months. What I remember most is feeling like I had so little control over anything in my life. Between Parkinson's and the fire, my confidence, my passion for life, and my work were tested almost to the breaking point.

I began picturing what I wanted my new home to look like. *What kinds of furniture would I buy? What feel did I want my home to have?* I wanted to create a space that felt like me that represented my taste, my heart; a place I could come home to and immediately feel comfortable. The process of rebuilding a home is long and made harder by contractors, delayed shipments, shoddy workmanship, and insurance companies, all while trying to make sense of why this happened. When I was finally able to move home, that feeling of security and safety took quite a bit of time to emerge. Being home was not the magic pill I had hoped it would be because I had to be comfortable in the new space. I had to make it mine. I had to learn to not jump every time a siren went by. With the help of a great therapist, I finally learned to feel at home in my home. I'm grateful that I have finally found the comfort and peace I deserve when I come home every day.

My Parkinson's remains a constant in my life. I have had progression in my symptoms, but nothing that I can't manage. I have an incredible medical team, the love and support of my family and friends, the work that drives me, and the hope that new treatments are on the horizon.

So, after all of this (and so much more, I have not shared), you may be wondering what I have learned from all of this heartache. I have learned that it is okay, 100 percent okay, to find joy and laughter in the midst of pain and uncertainty. I have learned that I have the right to feel happy; I have the right to take care of myself above all others; I have the right to be heard and supported and loved. I have learned that we don't get a break from difficult times and experiences. I've learned that the world doesn't stop because I'm going through something difficult. I have learned that I can make a difference in this world because of my experiences, because I not only keep going but I thrive and I find the light in every day. I truly believe and live my life with the philosophy that no matter how hard the day is, no matter how anxious I feel, no matter how much pain there may be in the world, I can find the light, the joy, and the hope in every day.

Therapeutic Summary

In this chapter, Stacey mentions a battle with anxiety throughout her adulthood, but also a devastating diagnosis of Parkinson's Disease and PTSD from losing her home in a fire. For Stacey, based on her description, one can only imagine how high her anxiety was in those first days of her diagnosis, watching her home burn, going through the rebuilding process, and then the anxiety that comes from PTSD triggers once she was back in her home. Stacey's medical diagnosis could have led to depression and grief in addition to her existing anxiety. And as she described, it took her awhile to not react and respond to the triggers from the fire once she got back into her home. PTSD consists of symptoms that include anxiety, depression, flashbacks, nightmares, reliving the trauma, and worried thoughts that the event will happen again, just to name a few.

Resources

- Parkinson's Foundation — parkinsons.org
- Counseling/Therapy — psychologytoday.com

STACEY STARTED HER CAREER in Child Welfare in 2011, spending ten years as a Case Coordinator and Dependency and Neglect Program Manager at Advocates for Children-(CASA). Stacey founded Elevating Connections in 2015 while still working at CASA and became the full-time executive director on May 1, 2022.

Stacey is a strong and passionate advocate for youth in foster care, especially separated siblings. Stacey truly enjoys educating stakeholders, families, and care providers about the importance of the sibling relationship and how every person involved with a family can help maintain and sustain the sibling bond.

Stacey is also passionate about helping youth post-emancipation find their voice and speak their truth through a variety of art modalities.

Stacey has two sisters who remind her every day how important the sibling relationship is to our overall well-being. She is an aunt to a niece and three nephews who are the absolute light of her life.

Keep Up with Stacey

elevatingconnections.org

Photo credits:
d20photography.com
empire.edu/cosmetology-schools/colorado/aurora-denver

A Journey to Completeness: Navigating the Adoption Maze for Our Little Miracle

Tammy Green Garner

During our girlhood, we envision our future selves, contemplating our desired professions, the spectacle of our weddings, the type of dwelling we'll inhabit, and the number of children that might grace our lives. Some of us go a step further, crafting names for the offspring we hope to welcome into the world. In my case, I had settled on Joshua David during my preteen years; however, the choice for a girl's name did not materialize until my adulthood, when I yearned for an Isabella.

Similar to many young girls, I belonged to that group who believed they knew, or at least thought they knew, what their future held. I meticulously laid out my aspirations: a career as an attorney, a grand wedding, a residence with ample space and a sizable yard, a couple of canine companions, and the joy of raising two children—one boy and one girl. Surprisingly, a significant portion of this vision manifested into reality. However, my journey took a detour from the legal profession, leading me into the realms of accounting and human resources. The elaborate wedding became a cherished memory, and our abode now stands proudly with a spacious yard, shared not only with my husband but also with four delightful dogs. The dream of having two children was realized with the arrival of two boys, who undeniably hold special places in my heart. Yet, a subtle longing persisted—a yearning for that missing puzzle piece, the little girl I had envisioned.

Conceiving has always been a challenge for me. The reasons behind this struggle remain elusive—perhaps stress played a role, or maybe there were underlying medical issues, or it could have been an entirely different factor. Things changed, during a time when I was preparing for blood work to initiate Accutane® (a drug known to pose risks to a developing fetus) treatment, the unexpected news that I was pregnant came to light. My doctor, cognizant of my husband Edward's deployment to Bosnia at the time, conveyed the startling revelation with a palpable concern in his voice. To alleviate his worries, I reassured him that Edward and I had rendezvoused in Budapest the month before for some rest and relaxation, prompting a visible sigh of relief from the concerned physician. The twist in the narrative unfolded eight months later when I joyfully welcomed my first child into the world—a son named Joshua David—marking a momentous occasion in my life at the age of twenty-five.

The desire for another child fueled our determination, prompting us to embark on the journey to expand our family with baby number two when the timing felt right. Little did we anticipate the arduous path that lay ahead.

After several years of unsuccessful attempts, we sought the expertise of a fertility doctor to navigate this challenging terrain. Months passed with a regimen of oral fertility drugs and, eventually, injectable fertility shots, yet success remained elusive.

The pivotal moment arrived when our fertility specialist delivered the disheartening news: conceiving naturally was no longer a viable option, and the prospect of in vitro fertilization (IVF) loomed on the horizon. The complex IVF process included the necessity of freezing sperm, a precursor to the eventual IVF procedure. Regrettably, the financial burden attached to IVF proved daunting, with a staggering cost of at least $26,000.00 and a mere 50 percent chance of success. This financial constraint forced us to shelve the prospect of IVF, leading to a period of waning optimism.

In a testament to Edward's unwavering support, he, understanding the magnitude of this dream, took the proactive step of freezing his sperm, holding onto the hope that someday we might navigate the challenges of IVF.

At eight years old, Joshua had become a central part of our lives, yet our aspirations for a larger family seemed as distant as they had been in the preceding years. It was during this period that the concept of adoption surfaced—a potential avenue to fulfill our desire for parenthood. Thoroughly researching the adoption process, engaging with agencies, and delving into the intricacies of adoption, we were confronted once again with a formidable hurdle: the substantial cost, exceeding $20,000.00, which remained beyond our financial means at that time.

After extensive deliberation and introspection, my husband and I arrived at a pivotal decision: Joshua, our beloved son, was enough to complete our family. Embracing this mindset, we consciously ceased to dwell on the unattainable, eliminating stress and forsaking any backward glances. In a curious turn of events, merely four months later, I found myself undergoing blood work in preparation for taking Accutane again, only to receive a familiar call from my doctor. The startling revelation: I couldn't proceed with Accutane due to pregnancy. Accutane seemed to wield an unexpected magic, as nine months later, our second child, Jayden Tyler, entered the world, when I was thirty-four years old.

Blessed with the miracle of Jayden—whose name, symbolizing "God has heard," resonated deeply with our sense of completion—we initially believed our family had reached its fulfillment. However, as the years unfolded, a yearning for another child persistently tugged at my heart. This desire, however, transcended the mere craving for additional offspring; it crystallized into an unwavering longing for a little girl. Despite having two cherubic boys who were the very essence of my joy, an unexplained void persisted, seemingly destined to be filled by the presence of a daughter. Motivated by this profound sentiment, we resolved to embark on another journey to expand our family once more.

Despite our efforts, conceiving proved elusive once again, and even the previously effective Accutane failed to bring the desired results. The diagnosis was polycystic ovary syndrome (PCOS), a condition known to complicate the journey to pregnancy. While not an insurmountable obstacle, the path forward was undeniably challenging. Faced with this reality, the prospect of another biological pregnancy appeared increasingly uncertain. Despite our initial resolution that our family was complete, the passage of a couple of years did little to quell the persistent ache within my soul—a void that seemed impossible to release.

With Jayden at the age of six and Joshua at fifteen, we began exploring potential paths, starting with the option of foster care. Foster care, we discovered, was a more financially viable route than adoption, and the state even provided financial support for caring for a child. Moreover, there was the possibility of adopting the foster child in some cases. However, the inherent challenge of fostering became evident: welcoming a child into your home, forging bonds within your family, establishing connections with your children, husband, family, and friends. While this could be a profound blessing for those fortunate enough to adopt the foster child, the potential for heartbreak loomed large for those less fortunate. The thought of investing weeks, months, or even years in nurturing a bond with a child, only to see them returned to their biological family was a heartbreak too agonizing to contemplate. Consequently, we opted against fostering, though the persistent void in my soul drove us back to consider adoption once again. With improved financial and emotional stability, we approached the decision-making process with a newfound sense of logic and tranquility.

After consulting with several adoption agencies, we decided to sign up with two agencies in the hope of adopting a newborn, with God's blessing. The decision to engage with two agencies stemmed from a practical consideration—the first agency, based out of state, did not conduct home studies in Colorado. Consequently, we needed to involve a Colorado agency, recommended by the out-of-state agency, to handle the home study. Since there was no additional cost associated with signing up with both agencies, we opted for dual-agency representation.

The adoption process commenced with the crucial home study, during which we outlined our preferences and specifications for the child we were hoping to adopt. Simultaneously, birth mothers reached out to the agency to initiate the adoption process for their unborn child—often several months prior to the baby's anticipated birth. The subsequent steps involved presenting potential adoptive parents to the birth parents, the birth parents selecting adoptive parents, reaching an agreement on living expenses for the birth mother, determining the adoptive parents' role during delivery, and deciding on the nature of the adoption (open, closed, or semi-open).

A noteworthy aspect of the adoption process is that if the birth mother decides to back out, she retains any living expenses provided by the adoptive parents. This underscores the importance of thorough research, asking pertinent questions, and relying on intuition for anyone contemplating the adoption journey.

In late August 2013, we underwent an intensive two-month home study process, which involved rigorous background checks, fingerprinting, home visits, and discussions with everyone residing in our home, including our boys. Our financials, tax returns, and personal references were scrutinized, accompanied by probing inquiries that delved into the most intimate aspects of our lives. As part of this comprehensive evaluation, we were required to complete a detailed four-page questionnaire outlining our preferences and limitations regarding potential adoptive children. This questionnaire covered aspects such as race, gender, disabilities, and even specific conditions like the loss of limbs. One pivotal aspect was whether we would be open to adopting a child with prenatal exposure to drugs or alcohol.

Initially, we expressed a preference for accepting an alcohol-exposed baby over a drug-exposed one, under the assumption that the recovery process might be less arduous for the former. However, the home study process proved to be an educational journey for us. We discovered that pediatricians generally preferred drug-exposed babies over alcohol-exposed ones. The rationale was that while drug-exposed infants might undergo withdrawal, their recovery was typically quicker compared to the potential long-term effects of fetal alcohol syndrome in alcohol-exposed babies. This revelation prompted us to reassess our stance on drugs and alcohol, leading to a shift in our preferences based on this newfound understanding.

Following an extensive examination of our lives, we received approval for adoption in early November 2013. Subsequently, we embarked on the task of creating a book featuring images of our family, home, pets, vacations, yard, and more. This personalized compilation served as a visual representation for potential birth parents, offering them a glimpse into our lives and helping them make an informed decision when selecting a family for their child.

It was conveyed to us that, due to our gender-specific preferences, it would likely take a minimum of a year before we received our first call from a potential birth parent.

On the Sunday preceding Thanksgiving, November 24, 2013, I received a call from our social worker. She informed us that she had emailed a photograph of a newborn baby girl born in Tulsa, Oklahoma, on Friday, November 22, 2013, who was available for adoption. Based on the questionnaire we had completed, the baby girl seemed to align with our criteria, and she asked if we would be interested in being considered as adoptive parents. Naturally, we enthusiastically agreed, leading to the submission of our family book, along with those of four other families, to the birth mother. Thus began the period of anticipation. The birth mother had until Tuesday, November 26, 2013, to decide which family she wished to entrust with the care of her baby.

We possessed two photographs of the baby and limited background information on the birth mother. Here's what we knew: the birth mother was of Hispanic/Caucasian descent; the birth father's identity remained unknown but was noted as African American; the birth mother engaged in weekly cocaine use during pregnancy. Surprisingly, the birth mother had not initially planned to put the baby up for adoption until after her birth. She suspected that the baby was not conceived with her boyfriend, attempting multiple times to induce a miscarriage. Due to her Catholic beliefs, abortion was not a viable option for her.

After the baby girl's birth, she received confirmation that the child was not her boyfriend's. Instead, she affirmed that the baby girl was the result of being raped. Aware of these challenging circumstances, we fervently prayed that she would choose us as the adoptive parents.

On Tuesday, November 26, 2013, around eight a.m., our phone rang, and it was the social worker. The birth mother was curious about why we hadn't pursued adoption all those years ago when we first considered it. My response was straightforward: we couldn't afford it at that time. "That seems reasonable," our social worker remarked, adding, "By the way, I think she is going to pick you. We will be in touch later today once a decision is made." If you know me, you know that upon hearing this news, I was already considering the baby as ours. I even created a collage from the pictures I had of her and gave her a name. The potential devastation would be immense if we were not chosen.

It was 2:30 in the afternoon, and we had just parked at Jayden's school for his Thanksgiving feast when our phone rang. The voice on the other end exclaimed, "How fast can you get to Oklahoma? She picked you!" Our excitement was palpable! We committed to heading out that evening, juggling the Thanksgiving feast, a last-minute baby-shopping spree (as we thought we had at least a year before anything would happen), and arranging care for our boys. After shopping, organizing, and packing, we hit the road at 7:30 p.m., drove through the night, and arrived in Tulsa at 5:30 a.m. on Wednesday, November 27, 2013. We did encounter a Kansas State Trooper for a faulty light, but he let us go when we explained we were rushing to Oklahoma to get our baby.

At just five days old, our baby girl was in the NICU due to traces of cocaine in her bloodstream, so we couldn't visit her until seven a.m., when NICU visiting hours began. At that moment, she had us at our "hello." Had we stuck to our initial decision of not accepting drug-exposed babies, we wouldn't be Isabella's parents today! The importance of answering those questions became abundantly clear.

After completing some paperwork, we were thrilled to bring Isabella Cheyenne back to our hotel that afternoon. However, there were still several steps before we could take her to Colorado. The birth mother needed to attend court to relinquish her rights, scheduled for the following Monday after Thanksgiving week. After the rights were terminated, we had to navigate an interstate child commerce compact, where Oklahoma released the child for her to cross state lines to Colorado—a process lasting about two weeks. Consequently, we resided in a hotel during this period while all the legal requirements were fulfilled. Approximately two weeks later, we received the green light to take Isabella home.

You might think this process went as smoothly, but it wasn't that easy. The birth mother arrived at court that Monday after Thanksgiving under the influence. It was crucial not to allow her to sign away her rights while impaired, as it could become grounds for her to contest the adoption later on. She needed to get sober, and a new court date had to be arranged.

Hearing this news devastated me. Our hearts sank; Isabella had been in our care for six days, and we had already formed a strong bond. Worries about the birth mother changing her mind consumed me. I cried like a baby and fervently prayed to God, pleading that she wouldn't reconsider. The relief came on Thursday, December 5, 2013, when the birth mother appeared in court, sober, and willingly signed away her rights. A week later, the necessary paperwork was finalized, allowing us to bring Isabella home.

You might wonder, doesn't the birth father have to sign away his rights, too? The answer is yes, but the details of this story are anything but brief. As part of the adoption process, the birth mother is required to provide the courts with a list of all her sexual partners within two years of her pregnancy. Fortunately, her list was concise, involving her then-boyfriend and the man who had assaulted her.

When the whereabouts of these men are known, the courts send documents requesting their signature to relinquish parental rights. The boyfriend, who was in jail for various offenses, including assault against the birth mother, received the paperwork. However, since the second man was unknown and never apprehended, an announcement was published in the paper regarding the birth of the baby girl. It called for anyone who might be the birth father to come forward and surrender his rights. Given the circumstances, this unidentified person was unlikely to step forward, as doing so could lead to charges of rape.

As long as no one contests the adoption, and after a specific period, the courts have the authority to relinquish any rights associated with the second man. That's precisely what happened—the courts released the rights for the second man, whoever he might be.

The situation with the boyfriend in jail presented a different set of challenges. Several months after bringing Isabella home, in February 2014, we learned that the incarcerated boyfriend was unwilling to surrender his rights. He asserted that Isabella was his child and expressed intentions to seek custody. The birth mother knew from the beginning that the boyfriend couldn't be the father because he was a white man with red hair, whereas Isabella displayed features of African American and Hispanic heritage.

Despite this, his contestation complicated the adoption process, disrupting our plans to finalize it in May 2014.

To address his claims, we had to engage in a lengthy process involving filing paperwork, undergoing DNA tests, and awaiting results. This period of uncertainty, lasting about four months, was emotionally taxing. Intellectually, I knew he couldn't be the birth father, and this issue would eventually be resolved. However, emotionally, the unknown was distressing. Isabella was my child, and I was determined not to let her go without a fight. The thought of him caring for an infant while in jail was concerning, and he claimed his mother would take care of Isabella until his release.

Finally, in August 2014, the DNA results confirmed he was not the birth father, and the necessary paperwork was filed to relinquish his rights. On October 10, 2014, we celebrated our "gotcha day." It was official—court documents stated that I am her mother and Edward is her father. No one could lay claim to her anymore; she was undeniably our daughter.

We've never had the chance to meet the birth mother, as she left the hospital just two days after Isabella was born. The adoption was closed, and she never had the opportunity to hold Isabella. Although she had no interest in meeting us, she requested a letter once a year around Isabella's birthday and some pictures. These letters are sent to the agency in Oklahoma, where she can pick them up.

Despite our requests for more letters and pictures to preserve for Isabella's future, she has only written back once, in the first year, and we haven't heard from her since. The birth mother is aware of Isabella's name, our names, and our boys' names, but she doesn't know our last name. She knows we reside in Colorado, and we're aware that Isabella has a half-sister who is two years older than her.

In the letters we send, we share details about our travels and adventures (which played a significant role in her choosing us), Isabella's participation in pageants and modeling, her various after-school activities like gymnastics, dance, soccer, and lacrosse, and highlight how intelligent she is. Our hope is that these letters provide the birth mother with a sense of peace, reassuring her that she made the right choice in selecting us as Isabella's mom and dad.

Having Isabella in our lives filled that void in my heart and soul. Although our family felt complete, I couldn't bring myself to remove our names from the original agency list (Isabella came from the Colorado agency). One day, after Isabella turned one, we received a call about another opportunity—an expectant birth mother, pregnant with a girl, wanted to give her up for adoption. We enthusiastically agreed to be considered.

This birth mother, located in Kentucky, had three sons. Over a month of conversation, she repeatedly brought up money, asking when we were going to send her some. This raised a red flag for me since discussions about finances are meant to be handled between the birth mother and the agency to avoid uncomfortable situations between birth mothers and adoptive families.

Eventually, my instincts told me she might be motivated by financial gain, and I worried she might change her mind after having the baby. Trusting my gut, we decided to back out of the adoption. It turned out to be the right decision for us, as she sent some unpleasant emails afterward. This experience reinforced the importance of following your instincts—it's almost never wrong.

Our journey was atypical. Typically, the adoption process is not swift, and the timeline varies based on individual preferences and when a birth mother selects a family. Despite the challenges we faced, we consider ourselves fortunate. Within two and a half weeks of being approved for adoption, we were chosen to become the parents of Isabella. Our good fortune extended to the fact that we had minimal expenses related to the birth mother, as she had not initially intended to place her baby up for adoption before Isabella was born. My family, heart and soul are now complete with my two boys and my little girl!

Therapeutic Summary

It is safe to say that during Tammy's journey, she and her family faced a lot of uncertainty, which can cause situational anxiety. The possibility of not being able to conceive can result in a sense of grief or loss. Women who are unable to conceive or have difficulty conceiving often experience a sense of grief around not being able to conceive and carry their own child. Some women may even experience levels of depression, anger, guilt, and/or shame during this time, which is common and part of the grief process. Much like the death of a loved one, women may mourn the loss of what could be or what could have been when experiencing fertility issues.

Finding a counselor experienced in fertility issues as well as grief and loss can be helpful when navigating through fertility issues.

Therapeutic Resources

- American Fertility Association — theafa.org
- North American Council on Adoptable Children — nacac.org
- American Society for Reproductive Medicine — reproductivefacts.org

A Journey to Completeness

I'm Tammy Green Garner, and my heart beats for my family. With two level-headed boys, one spirited girl, and a devoted husband, our home is alive with love. Our four playful pups complete our picture of happiness. Whether it's the warmth of the sun on my face or the sensation of sand beneath my toes, simple joys fill me with contentment. Traveling ignites my soul, taking me from my roots in Maryland to adventures overseas, in the Southeast, and eventually to Colorado. Though miles may separate us, my heart remains connected to my family back home. Dreaming of Australia, I yearn to embrace a koala one day. As I embark on my newfound love for reading, I embrace the journey ahead. From staying updated on pop culture to immersing myself in current events, curiosity drives me forward.

Professionally, as both director of finance and chief people officer, I am empowered to enhance business efficiency and foster the growth of our exceptional team. Driven by a relentless passion for learning, I embrace every opportunity for self-improvement.

Keep Up with Tammy

rockymountainbooksandbalances.com

Photo credits:
billymontanaimages.com
empire.edu/cosmetology-schools/colorado/aurora-denver

Follow our movement:

reigningresilientqueens.com

Embracing True Beauty: A Journey of Resilience and Purpose

Whitley Nabintu Marshall

My early years were marked by adversity. I was born in an upscale suburb of Chicago into a charismatic family of dreamers who were often running from their problems through workaholism and escapism. For as long as I can remember, my mother was the sole provider of our family. She worked long hours each day. My dad would escape his self-loathing shame of failure after losing his job by reading fantasy and mystery novels, staying at home with us kids, while depressed and avoiding responsibility. We were regularly living outside our means, being threatened with eviction nearly every month, and arguments grew increasingly explosive.

We moved eight times. Then, following the separation of my parents while living in Texas, my mom got a job back in Chicago, and she took us with her, leaving my dad in Texas. As we drove away, my body sank, as my heart was crushed. My safe person was gone. None of us realized in that moment how my shattered twelve-year-old heart would trigger a spiral of self-destructive patterns, impacting us all.

Before my 21st birthday, I faced multiple near-death experiences, two full-body recoveries, was admitted into and graduated from drug rehab, moved across the country, experienced a brief period of homelessness, and battled food insecurity. Each of these experiences played a role in the woman I am and the life I lead. In trying to escape the pain, I was missing the lessons. As I peeled back the layers of conformity, conditioning, and fears, I came face-to-face with my addictive patterns, my wounded inner child, with God, and met my true authentic self. Each setback became an opportunity for growth and empowerment.

Finding Purpose Through Creativity and Activism

Driven by a passion to create positive change, I channeled my experiences into activism, art, and service to others. My personal and familial healing journey began after my darkest hour—using anything I could get my hands on to attempt suicide. I am grateful every day for the coping tools I was given in those years, for the breaking point that taught me how to break free and how to ask for help. I found that serving others is the greatest way to serve the soul.

Art possesses a profound ability to touch the depths of our being, where words often fail to reach. Engaging in the creative process offers a sanctuary for our minds to confront the toughest challenges we face. With tools as simple as brushes and paint, or just a pen, we can confront and even reframe our struggles, finding solace and clarity in the act of expression.

What did finding purpose look like for me? After receiving multiple blood transfusions from a near-fatal car accident, I later worked for the American Red Cross Biomedical Services for over sixteen years. Collecting lifesaving blood products was a job that gave me security after facing homelessness at nineteen. For seven of those years, I also worked for the same teen shelters I once received services from. I found balance with my work life through my arts. For five years, I sang in two bands and delved into songwriting. When life shifted plans, I was recruited into a dance company and became a co-director, while also performing with a Rwandan cultural troupe. I later founded the Rhythm Rebels Dance Collective. Having lived and traveled across the country as well as abroad in East Africa, I have a unique perspective with diverse cultural and creative influences.

Embracing True Beauty: My Journey Toward Self-Acceptance and Empowerment

The pandemic era was another opportunity for resilience. So many things happened: my dance gigs dropped off, my dad died shortly after testing positive for COVID-19, and then I got a long COVID infection that significantly limited my ability to work long hours. I decided to step further into my talents and enroll in a personal training and nutrition course. I have learned firsthand the incredible healing power of nutrition and exercise, and the importance of forming healthy habits that last. In my adult life, I have been both a size two and a size eighteen. It was these heaviest and lowest breaking points that taught me to intentionally hold compassion and love for the body I am in, no matter the size, shifting my mindset from *looking* a certain way to *treating myself* a certain way. All this led me to coach others of all abilities to do the same.

Bridging Communities Through Art and Culture

Combining my passions for expanding beauty standards and bridging communities through the arts, I launched *Artlovelifestyle Magazine* and Productions to use fashion as a tool for empowerment. Through *Artlovelifestyle Magazine* and Artlovelifestyle Attire, I aim to expand beauty standards and elevate underrepresented voices in the fashion industry. Art has the power to transcend barriers and unite hearts.

Navigating the World of Pageantry

My journey in pageantry has been transformative. As the first openly pansexual International Mrs. USA, I've shattered stereotypes and championed authenticity, but I didn't initially believe I fit the mold. What I have learned is there is no mold, that every woman is unique and striving to be their best selves while building sisterhood. Pageantry has provided me with a platform to advocate for diversity, equity, and inclusion while also challenging traditional beauty norms. With each crown and accolade, I've used my voice to inspire and empower others.

Building a Legacy of Compassionate Leadership

Through my work as a coach and mentor, I strive to cultivate compassionate leaders who embody true beauty. Together with my collaborator, Patrick Kiruhura, I cofounded the World Roots Culture Exchange and spearheaded the Compassionate Leadership Project. Our shared mission to cultivate a global network of compassionate leaders through storytelling, cultural arts, and community service embodies my unwavering commitment to creating a more compassionate world. The Compassionate Leadership Project empowers people to lead with empathy, authenticity, and resilience. By nurturing the next generation of leaders, I hope to create a ripple effect of positive change in the world.

Empowering Others through Resilience

My journey is not just about personal triumphs but about empowering others to embrace their own resilience and authenticity. Whether through coaching, modeling, or activism, I strive to bring hope and inspiration for those facing adversity. Together, we can rewrite the narrative of what it means to be truly beautiful.

Conclusion: A Legacy of Compassion

Life is a mosaic of diverse experiences, each fragment a reflection of our unique journey. From the depths of adversity to the heights of achievement, I aspire to embody the essence of true beauty—a beauty that transcends physical appearance and emanates from the depths of the human spirit. As a champion for inclusivity and compassion, I hope the ripple effect impacts generations to come. The greatest gift we can give is the gift of compassion.

Therapeutic Summary

In this chapter, Whitley briefly acknowledges the pain and difficulties of having her parents' divorce during her adolescence, struggling with some sort of addiction, being homeless, facing food insecurity, and attempting suicide, in addition to nearly losing her life as the result of a serious car accident. As Whitley mentions, we oftentimes try to deal with difficulties in life by running from them. Sometimes, running from our problems means running to addiction, as was the case here. As a result of all she was dealing with and had gone through, Whitley found herself surviving a suicide attempt. Early trauma, such as the divorce or separation of parents, can lead to feelings of abandonment, isolation, and loneliness for children, which in turn can lead to depression, drug or alcohol use, and other issues. As a result of experiencing homelessness, facing food insecurity, addiction, and possible depression, suicide may have seemed like her only way out at the time. Research shows that those experiencing homelessness are actually ten times more likely to complete suicide than other population cohorts.

Resources

- National Healthcare for the Homeless Counsel - nhchc.org
- Salvation Army - salvationarmyusa.org
- Substance Abuse and Mental Health Services Administration - samhsa.gov
- National Suicide Hotline — Call/Text 988
- Counseling/Therapy - psychologytoday.com

WHITLEY NABINTU MARSHALL is a multifaceted dynamic force in the realms of art, fashion, dance, and activism. As Mrs. Florida Elemental, North America's World Top Model, and the first openly pansexual International Mrs. USA (2022), she embodies resilience, creativity, and authenticity, using her platform to champion diversity and inclusivity. Her journey, defined by surviving near-death experiences, overcoming food insecurity, and facing homelessness before the age of twenty-one, stands as a powerful testament to transforming adversity into purpose.

As the CEO and editor-in-chief of *Artlovelifestyle Magazine* and the creative mind behind Artlovelifestyle Attire, Whitley Nabintu Marshall is on a mission to redefine beauty standards and lead the charge for sustainable fashion. Through her initiatives like True Beauty NYFW, Flowers that Feed Art and Fashion Showcase, World Roots Culture Exchange, and the Compassionate Leadership Project, she creates vital platforms that elevate underrepresented voices and celebrate compassion, resilience, diversity, and authenticity, both in print and on the runway.

Through Mind Body Compassion Coaching, Whitley empowers her clients to cultivate authenticity, compassionate leadership, and holistic well-being. Her transformative approach blends mindfulness, self-discovery, and legacy building, offering tailored guidance for those in pageantry, fashion, and beyond.

In addition to her coaching and editorial work, Whitley leads the Rhythm Rebels Dance Collective, captivating audiences worldwide. Her impact has been recognized by prestigious publications like *Vogue* and *Forbes*, and she's received accolades such as the Director's Leadership Award and the Inspirational Woman Award. Whitley's journey invites others to embrace their unique path with determination and purpose.

Keep Up with Whitley

https://linktr.ee/artlovelifestyle

Photo credits:
d20photography.com
empire.edu/cosmetology-schools/colorado/aurora-denver

Follow our movement:

reigningresilientqueens.com

Dare to Be Different

Whitney Watts Hays

"**Since I don't look like** every other girl, it takes a while to be okay with that. To be different. But different is good." —Serena Williams

Growing up, my mom always told me that being different was good. I liked to stand out a little bit. In a room full of girls wearing white, I rocked the orange dress. And when I joined the marching band, I was a drummer. I just wanted to have fun. I never expected a saying to become so much more to my life.

In 2020, the world was turned upside down by the COVID-19 pandemic. Everyone went home. Kids learned from home. Adults worked from home. It forced us to slow down, and it pushed families into spending more time together (pleasant or not). But my 2020 journey got a plot twist that would change my life forever.

Having more time at home gave me an opportunity to focus on some personal goals. My husband and I started working out together. The family went for walks after dinner. I lost twenty pounds and was the strongest I had ever been. I felt so good in my body. And in this time of family bliss, my husband and I thought it wouldn't be a bad idea to add one more kid. At the time, my other girls were seven and four years old.

I noticed some changes after losing weight, and one thing was a marble-sized lump on the outside of my left breast. I had an appointment coming up with my doctor for my annual checkup, so I decided I would talk to him about the lump and get cleared to go for baby number three.

My doctor said I was healthy and fine to give the baby thing a go. But he did want to check out the lump. He set me up for an ultrasound and a mammogram and connected me with a general surgeon. Once the surgeon got my images, his office called to schedule me for a biopsy to see what it was. My husband and I started thinking that maybe this is something we need to deal with first before a baby, so we said if it didn't happen that month, we would put it on hold.

Two weeks off birth control, and I got a positive test! I couldn't believe that it happened so fast. I went in for my biopsy with hopes it was a calcium lump that could be cut out. But at nine a.m. on Halloween, the surgeon called and said my lump was cancerous.

Everything from there was just a whirlwind of doctor's appointments and plans. My oncologist explained that my tumor was made up of estrogen and progesterone. First we needed to remove the breast with the tumor, then we would remove tubes and ovaries later. This would help my body stop producing the hormones, and then I would also be on a hormone blocking medication for 5-10 years. So, then I was asked if I wanted to just remove one breast or both. I jumped to the decision to do both because I did not want to be a one-boobed wonder. Ha! Then I could continue my pregnancy as planned and start hormone treatments after her birth. Yes, another girl!

At seven weeks pregnant, I prepared for surgery. They started prepping me, and then the surgeon said he did not want to keep me under anesthesia for the length of time required to remove both breasts. So, he was going to only take the breast with the tumor and would remove the other one after the baby was born. The irony was present. It happened so fast that I didn't quite grasp how that would change in the next nine months.

Not only was I about to start showing I was pregnant, but I have just one, off-centered boob. I had received a prosthetic boob for the other side to make things look more even. But it was weird and uncomfortable, especially once summer hit. And the not-so-funny thing is that all those pregnancy hormones went into one boob, which ended up being huge. The prosthetic couldn't keep up toward the end. I just kept looking forward to being a little more symmetrical after the baby.

Baby number three came out healthy and strong. Then it was time to tackle the rest of this cancer plan. The next surgery was to remove the right breast, my tubes, and ovaries. I just wanted to get it over with so that I could get back home with my new baby. I never knew how hard the journey would be from that point forward.

Once I got into a routine with the baby, I finally had the chance to really let what all I had been through sink in. And now I was looking in the mirror with baby weight, a deflated tummy, and a flat chest. It was harder than I thought it would be. I had to change my clothes. I had styles that didn't look right anymore. But I tried to look on the positive side. I didn't have to wear a bra ever again, and I could wear open-back shirts.

The bare nakedness of my chest was startling. I started to look at tattoos that other women had gotten to cover their scars or chests. I found a local tattoo artist who was a woman who designed mine for me. I told her that I wanted something that was like a bralette. I wanted to feel not so naked. I wanted to add something feminine. And boy, did she deliver. My chest piece was such an awesome way for me to turn something around. The best thing about it was that I couldn't feel most of the tattoo process.

So now I was feeling better about my chest, but I was still holding on to so much baby weight. I had also started my hormone-blocking medication, which makes it so much harder to reach those goals. Sometimes, I would stare at the mirror and say, *You have three beautiful children. You survived cancer while pregnant. You are taking care of a young family that needs you so much. And this body provides.* I had to take those negative thoughts and turn them around for my benefit. I was going to wear this badge on my chest, and I wasn't going to be any less of a woman for it.

And I got back to the gym. Well, I got together with some friends and started a gym. A women's only gym. A gym to build muscles and community. I was not a businessperson, but I was a believer in what a group of women can do together. We built a gym where women from all walks of life came together to exercise. They encouraged one another. They vented to one another. They supported each other through the rough patches. Surrounding myself with strong women has allowed me to grow so much as a person. I also grew muscles and confidence. I even signed up and ran a 5-kilometer run in my town, supporting local women with breast cancer. I will not say it was fun, because I am not a runner. However, I said I was going to run it, and I did.

The realization of my own strengths has pushed me so much further in the last few years. It honestly sucks that I had to battle something like cancer to come to these realizations. But now I have found my voice and I have found the woman inside me. The woman that is a warrior. The woman that was always there but has now come to the surface. I have pushed myself further than I ever had and done things that I may have never done prior. I will continue to push myself because strong women do strong things.

So, yes, I am different from most women around me, and realizing that being different is okay was such a freeing moment for me. Some days, I wake up and feel like a badass. Like I have conquered a mountain and am stronger for it. Some days, I stare at the mirror and grieve a little for the me I lost. I know that embracing my body is something that will come with time. But for now, I know that it is okay to be different. Different is good.

As Allison Rushby said, "The world would be a boring place if everyone was the same." So go out today and add some color to the world, add some beauty, and make your life and the lives of those around you a work of art. Break the mold and be great, be different—it is okay, and more times than not, it is what makes you, me, and the rest of this world *so* beautiful.

Therapeutic Summary

In this chapter, Whitney experienced an unexpected breast cancer diagnosis amidst a pandemic and pregnancy. This would have been more than enough to send some people into a tailspin of fear, anxiety, and depression. For Whitney, the pregnancy kept her almost in survival mode, which, at the time, was a good thing. She focused on what needed to be done and did it. However, after the baby was born, the reality of her situation could have led to postpartum depression and anxiety, and she did mention her experience with grief. In a situation like this, it would be understandable to experience grief around the loss of a part of your body, especially for a woman, a part of her body that society says makes her a woman. Feeling some anger and sadness and experiencing some level of depression can be common in a situation like this, as well as a negative impact on self-esteem and self-worth.

Resources

- American Cancer Society — cancer.org
- Susan G Komen Foundation — komen.org
- Postpartum Depression Hotline — 833-TLC-MAMA (833-852-6262)
- Therapy/Counseling — psychologytoday.com

WHITNEY WATTS HAYS grew up in the Birmingham area in Alabama. She completed her Bachelor of Science degree from Athens State University in Behavioral Science. She then went on to receive her Master of Science in Continuing Education Counseling/Psychology from the University of West Alabama. Whitney taught adjunct psychology and sociology classes at two different community colleges in Alabama for ten years. Whitney is married to Justin Hays, and they have three daughters, Kaitlyn, Aubrey, and Eleanor. In 2017 her family relocated to Jackson, Tennessee. In 2020, Whitney was diagnosed with breast cancer while pregnant with her third baby. After her cancer journey, Whitney took her love for helping others to the gym. She partnered with Carrie Ralph and created Fortress Women's Gym. This gym created a safe space for strong women to come and support one another. Whitney enjoys heavy lifting and hanging out at home.

Keep Up with Whitney

https://linktr.ee/whitneywattshays

Photo credits:
instagram.com/folklorephotography1
lushblowdryandbeautyco.com

Follow our movement:

reigningresilientqueens.com

Acknowledgments

They say it takes a village to raise a child. Well, I say it takes a village to do anything. Period!

This project has been over two years in the making, and I could not have gotten this far without the help and support of so many people—along with the challenges, strife, and disbelief from those who doubted me. Both the encouragement and the obstacles have driven me to where I am today and helped keep me balanced in my worldview.

First and foremost, I want to dedicate this book to my children, who must go first on this list of thank-yous. We have been through so much together, and in many ways, we have grown up together. That's one of the downfalls of being such a young mom. If I had known the type of healing I needed to do, I might have waited to have you. Then again, being told I wouldn't have kids unless I had them young—and selfishly wanting children so badly—if I had waited, I wouldn't have had you. I don't want to imagine what might have been if I had made a different choice. Even through the unbelievable events we've endured together, I am so grateful for the relationship we have today. I fought so hard, saying, "My kids are not my friends. I am their parent!" your whole lives, but now I can honestly say you are not just my kids, but you are truly my friends. I love how we interact, and I enjoy listening to your views on the world through your lens. Watching you grow up and become the people you are today has been the greatest blessing in my life. I cannot fathom where I would be without your love and support. I am incredibly grateful and so proud of the humans you are!

To my leadership team—each of you has been nothing short of amazing! Not only have you dedicated time for meetings, been my listening ears, and served as voices of reason, but each one of you has also truly provided immense value in getting us to where we are today.

Our Queen of Inner Beauty, Heather Brooke, dedicated time and effort to read each chapter and provide a therapeutic summary, along with tools and resources to help our readers find the support they need based on the stories they resonate with. I had a wild idea one day and called her up to tell her I wanted to see how we could partner up to offer free or reduced mental health services to our community. Not only was she on board, but she also said she already had that calling for herself as well and would be more than happy to partner with us! Her nonprofit, My Pain His Purpose Ministries, is now a partner, and we couldn't be more excited! Heather, you are so valuable. Thank you for being who you are and who God called you to be!

Our Queen of Community, Karleen Wagner, has introduced me to so many of the women who are part of this book, and so many others, giving me the opportunity to learn about their heartfelt stories of triumph and adversity. As if that gift alone wasn't enough, she has organized and run our virtual monthly meetings to help build our community, dedicates time to grow our social media group, and reached out to each of the queens one-on-one so they know they have a team of women who care about them as a whole. Karleen has also been my balance when I get my wild ideas. I cannot tell you how much I appreciate you for being exactly who you are!

Our Queen of Redemption, Kalena Rodriguez, opened up her organization, Built to Recover, to partner with us so that together we can help those in recovery receive added support and resources to live their best lives free of addiction. She also recently opened an online school, Loyal Beginnings, for kids who don't fit into the traditional high school environment, giving them the opportunity to earn their degree. Additionally, her nonprofit organization, K. Project Freedom, provides incarcerated individuals with the tools to reintegrate into society and write their success stories to inspire and uplift others. Kalena, thank you for keeping your promise to God, being my friend, business partner, and un-biological sister, and for providing such valuable programs to the community!

Thank you to my original queens (OQs)—Dorie McCleskey, Heather Brooke, Karleen Wagner, Kalena Rodriguez, Tammy Green Garner, and Emily Moore—I appreciate each of you for staying with this since the beginning and never losing faith in me, my God-given determination, or the knowledge that this was going to happen because it is a calling, not just a whim.

Thank you to all of the author queens—Dorie McCleskey, Gabby Gonzales, Heather Brooke, Jenna Janisch, Kalena Rodriguez, Karleen Wagner, Laura Farley, Lauren Jurkas, Marta Spirk, Shantelle Bridges, Stacey Sanders, Tammy Green Garner, Whitney Nabintu Marshall, and Whitney Hays. Thank you for your vulnerability in sharing your stories with the world, and for your unwavering love, support, patience, grace, and kindness. None of this would be possible without each of you!

As this anthology book was transforming into a movement, I had a vision to have a theme song. The first person who came to mind was Marta Spirk. We had followed each other on social media and supported each other's endeavors, but we hadn't met in person yet, so I wasn't sure how to approach the subject. I asked Karleen to talk to her, as they knew each other from Marta's anthology book, *The Empowered Woman*. Marta was more than happy to take what I wrote and make it better, as well as work with music producer Ian Escario in London to accomplish the mission. Just the samples have made me cry every time I listen to them. I cannot wait to hear the final product. Marta, thank you for bringing one of your many talents to the community, beauty!

Lauren Jurkas, you were brought to us through a woman who is no longer part of this movement, but she was the vehicle God used to bring us one of the most encouraging, loving, and amazing cheerleaders we could have asked for! The way you show up for RRQ as a whole is nothing short of a blessing! I am so grateful that you answered the calling and joined our team. I see how you like, comment, share, and send messages to all the ladies. You have made such a difference in this project with your bright light and energy. Thank you for being you!

Erin Baer is a big supporter and great friend! When things didn't work out with the last publishing company, I felt discouraged and unsure of my next move. All I knew was that I *had* to figure something out and move this thing forward. She jumped right in and introduced me to Amy Collette, who had a similar story to mine and opened her own publishing company as a result. I am grateful for this connection, as well as Amy's grace, kindness, knowledge, and patience throughout this process.

Christine Beckwith is a powerhouse of a woman and so inspiring to many people, including myself. I am grateful that she answered her calling and shows up as the woman she is in all aspects! Christine, thank you for being you and for agreeing to write your very heartfelt foreword for this book. I was touched when you agreed, and at a loss for words when I read your thoughtful remarks.

Dean Kokorus with Competitive Edge MMA has not only been encouraging and provided ideas on how we can partner up and help each other provide much-needed services and resources to the community but has also opened up his amazing space for RRQ to hold events and spread our message to those who need our services. Dean, thank you for all you do to help people build their confidence and protect themselves, especially the children.

In 2023, I was seeking a sign from God—something to truly shake up my life. Many things ended up happening that year to do just that. The beginning of which started with an unexpected invitation to a concert by a renowned rapper and entrepreneur I've admired for years. Though skeptical about the promised backstage access, the night unfolded miraculously.

Not only did I enjoy an incredible show from backstage, but I also had

Acknowledgments

the privilege of meeting the artist after the show. We engaged in a profound conversation during which he shared invaluable advice, emphasizing the importance of trusting one's instincts in business and personal matters. It felt as though God was speaking directly through him. This encounter deepened my respect for him as an artist and a genuine human being and solidified my admiration.

His bodyguard (my now contact) invited me to another concert the following year at Red Rocks. While I didn't interact with the artist due to his tight schedule, I was able to have a meaningful conversation with his bodyguard. Our discussion covered various topics, from life to business, offering me fresh perspectives and reaffirming the artist's humane approach to his work and relationships.

These experiences underscored the remarkable alignment and loyalty between the artist and his bodyguard, illuminating the reasons behind their long-standing partnership. I am immensely grateful for these moments of mentorship and guidance, as they have significantly influenced my journey. Truly, I see God's hand in bringing these influential figures into my life at a pivotal time.

Sometimes, you have experiences or meet people without fully understanding the reason, but you somehow know it is all part of God's plan for your life and theirs. Scott Craig, thank you for providing me with a different perspective and insight, helping me work on some unhealed parts of myself I didn't realize needed healing, and for all your help in creating the logo and graphics for our movement. You have a bright future in your author, speaking, and art career. Thank you for showing up as who you were meant to be in this world.

Jess Sidoti, we met and bonded over experiences and opportunities that were once in a lifetime. I am grateful we had each other to persevere and navigate some of the most unforeseen moments while we were in Kansas City. Thank you for being so caring and loving, touching my heart, and giving me memories I will never forget!

Devin Frost, talk about an unconventional bestie friendship birthed through a "WTF just happened?" time in our lives! When we met, neither of us expected to click the way we did, but we just did. I am so grateful to have met you. You have provided me belief in myself, support, advice, laughs, and have made fun of me in the only way I would expect from an un-biological brother. You even managed to have my kiddos think you are absolutely great, and they are pretty skeptical of people—especially my daughter. Thank you for being who you are, sending all the memes, GIFs, and reels, and showing up the way you do! You have made a difference!

Mitchell Harlan, you sir, have been a challenge and a blessing all in one human! You are a big part of that "woo woo BS" that happened this past year—and in my life in general—and certainly part of God's plan to get me to see things a bit differently and refine the way I show up for myself in life. I appreciate all of our talks, our partnership, and the plans we have for the future! Let's do this!

Steven Eurioste, thank you for your understanding, kindness, and unwavering support. It is rare to find a person with as kind and pure a heart as yours. Anyone who meets you can see right away how much you care about the world, especially the children. Thank you for answering your call and showing up the way you do with "Curiosity and Encouragement."

Shannon Glorioso, GIRL!!! YOU have been such a blessing in my life. Coming to my rescue so many times—100+ degree fevers, broken wrists, undergarment emergencies (haha!)—you are an unsung hero of sorts. I'm truly grateful for our connection. God/the universe/higher power knew EXACTLY what I needed when we creepily caught eyes with each other from across the room. I love how someone right now is reading this going, "What?"

Joni Young, you were an unexpected meeting from an unexpected place during an unexpected time in my life, but in the short time we have known each other, you have made a giant impact! You have shown up for so many people in your life and have not always received the recognition you deserve! You are a wonderful woman, mother, wife, grandma, and un-biological mom. Thank you for being a real one—it's a beautiful thing to have had the opportunity to know you.

Cheryl Braunschweiger, you have always checked in on me when I needed it most, believed in me, supported me, given me hard truths, and been a great example to not just me but all the women you take under your wing. Thank you for showing up the way you do—you truly make a difference in this world.

Laura Curtis, thank you to you and your wonderful hubby, David Tatham, for being great photographers and sharing your gift with me through the years and now with the RRQ queens—helping them see their beauty through our eyes! You have also been a catalyst in helping me overcome something that was holding me back in many ways. Because of you, I was able to free myself just a little bit more. Your support, partnership, and caring nature are genuinely appreciated.

Andy Huling, thank you for answering the Facebook group message and jumping in to help this movement by taking incredibly flattering and beautiful pictures of a woman who truly deserves to see her beauty! Whitney Hays was the only queen unable to come to Colorado, and I wanted to be sure I found someone who would make her feel special and like she wasn't missing out. You certainly stepped up to the plate and allowed her natural beauty to shine through your photos.

Billy Montana, we connected through our crazy and memorable photo shoots with *Supermodels Unlimited Magazine*. We have proven that incredible and beautiful art can still be magical even when "shit happens" (lmfao!). Thank you for your belief in this movement, your friendship, your partnership, and for helping the people in our lives see their true beauty through your lens. We have truly helped so many people, and the proof of concept is in our testimonials of our impact! Here's to more memories and making even more of an impact.

Whitley Nabintu Marshall, our bonding experience when you came to Colorado is truly one for the books. Getting to know you more and how you see the world was such a blessing and solidified why you have received all the accolades you have. You were put on this earth to make a difference, and you are absolutely doing just that! Thank you for stepping up during photoshoot day and being my day coordinator, a leader queen, an encouraging soul, and for helping the ladies see their unique beauty through our eyes! It is what you do in general, but I didn't realize I needed you the way I did. You just stepped in so seamlessly that I couldn't be more grateful! Also, thank you for providing a spread in your *Artlovelifestyle Magazine* for RRQ's first official publication!

Tiffany Jay with Empire Beauty School, thank you so much for answering the call, seeing the vision, and taking action to partner up, allow your students to help their resumes and gain exposure, as well as help women see their beauty and make them feel like the queens they are! I cannot wait to see where this partnership goes nationally! Let's go! Let's grow!

Carisa Bosworth, you have watched me grow up in a lot of ways and have been one of my biggest supporters, biggest cheerleaders, and oldest friends! I am so grateful for you never giving up on me and always helping me where you could. I value you in my life. Although we don't spend as much time together, we haven't grown apart in our hearts, and I am truly so grateful for that. We can just pick up where we left off like it was nothing. You are my family! Thank you for being exactly who you are!

Marcella Neverman, your support and nonjudgmental friendship have meant so much to me through the years. You have provided an ear when I needed it, proper eyewear I didn't know I needed through your expertise and amazingly fashionable eyewear you have at 20/20 EyeVenue, and some great advice I may or may not have always wanted, Lol. I love your heart and your honesty. Thank you for being that woman so many other women need.

Grandmother, thank you for being the one adult I needed in my life. Thank you for being an example of a powerful and hardworking woman who is loving and caring but takes no guff from those who lack self-awareness. Thank you for showing me that no matter what you have been through in your life, you can overcome, push through, and achieve greatness! I am, in part, the woman I am today because of you!

Mr. Timothy Phillips, wow, we have certainly been through a lot over the years—ups, downs, and everything in between. When I first started this journey of building Reigning Resilient Queens with another publisher under a different book title, I wrote about how we met from my perspective, hoping it would help us connect and strengthen our relationship. Although things didn't turn out as I had hoped or envisioned when we first met, I believe our meeting was meant to happen, all part of God's plan, and it has profoundly impacted both of our lives in many ways. Your presence in my life has taught me to bet on myself, regardless of how others respond, and to let go of expectations—whether in relationships, partnerships, or any other aspect of life. I know we both did and continue to do the best we can, and through our conversations and healing, it's clear that we genuinely want the best for each other, even if that means not being together. I appreciate the fact that we've seen the ugliest parts of each other and yet know that we never intended to cause harm, even though we've hurt each other along the way. Despite the pain, we've also healed parts of ourselves that needed healing to become who we are today. I don't know what the future holds, but I am grateful for your contributions—both good and bad—that have helped shape me into the woman I am now. You are such a significant part of my journey, and I cannot thank you enough. I believe that one day, our full story, in all its complexity, will help others when the time is right. For now, simply put, thank you for all the moments and memories.

Thank you, little Genesis, for never giving up! You are smart, you are worthy, and you are beautiful. Thank you for always doing the best you can, and when you learn better, thank you for striving to do better!

Thank you, God, for giving me this vision since I was a little girl, for orchestrating the events, people, and experiences that have brought this movement to life, and for instilling in me whatever it is that keeps me going, even when I've come close to giving up or wanted to so badly. This journey has been anything but easy, but it has been worth every moment—and it's only the beginning!

Thank you to those who are holding this book in your hand and for all those who are supporting our movement in one way or another. Together, we can do more and help more people feel less alone in this world!